earning Exchange LRC
0151 252-3769

Real
Listening & Speaking 4
with answers

Miles Craven

CAMBRIDGE
UNIVERSITY PRESS

CAMBRIDGE UNIVERSITY PRESS
Cambridge, New York, Melbourne, Madrid, Cape Town, Singapore,
São Paulo, Delhi, Dubai, Tokyo

Cambridge University Press
The Edinburgh Building, Cambridge CB2 8RU, UK

www.cambridge.org
Information on this title: www.cambridge.org/9780521705905

First published 2008
4th printing 2010

Printed in the United Kingdom at the University Press, Cambridge

A catalogue record for this publication is available from the British Library

ISBN 978-0-521-70590-5 Paperback with answers and audio CD
ISBN 978-0-521-70591-2 Paperback without answers

Contents

Map of the book

Unit number	Title	Topic	How to ...
Social and Travel			
1	**How's it going?**	Socializing	• start up a conversation and make small talk • develop and maintain a conversation • understand when someone is being ironic • use intonation to indicate emotions
2	**I'm looking for a camera**	Shopping	• ask about products in detail • negotiate and get a good deal • return an item to a shop and give an explanation
3	**I need to see a doctor**	Healthcare	• enquire about and register for health services • understand a doctor's diagnosis • use stress to correct any important misunderstandings
4	**What's the problem?**	Living away from home	• describe everyday problems and speculate about causes and consequences • give advice and make strong recommendations • explain the consequences of particular actions
5	**What a lot of red tape!**	Bureaucracy	• ask about official procedures • understand official processes • be concise and to the point when answering questions
6	**What a great view!**	Sightseeing	• show visitors around your home town • talk about places of interest • ask about attractions in a city • make strong recommendations
Work and Study			
7	**I'd appreciate it**	Requesting services	• understand detailed requirements • make polite requests and explain what you want • interupt politely and ask for help • specify requirements and justify your reasons
8	**This is your office**	Organizations and people	• understand and explain company structures • understand roles and responsibililties • talk about your role and responsibilities • describe personal qualities and strengths

Work and Study

Acknowledgements

The author would like to thank all the Cambridge University Press team involved in the development of *Real Listening & Speaking 4* for their commitment, enthusiasm and outstanding support; especially Noírín Burke, Roslyn Henderson, Caroline Thiriau, Linda Matthews and Martine Walsh. Very special thanks also to Sheila Dignen and Claire Thacker for their excellent editing, and to Bell International for the use of their wonderful facilities. Finally, I would like to thank Jessica for her love, patience and support, which make all things possible.

The author and publishers are grateful to the following reviewers for their valuable insights and suggestions:

Kathryn Alevizos, UK
Steve Banfield, UK
Barbara Gardner, UK
Nigel Daly, Taiwan
Rosie Ganne, UK
Hebe Gomez, Spain
Peter Gray, Japan
Jessie Mackay, Spain
Dr Zbigniew Mozejko, Poland
Paul Seligson, UK
Raymond Sheehan, UAE
Rui da Silva, Korea
Wayne Trotman, Turkey

The authors and publishers acknowledge the following sources of copyright material and are grateful for the permissions granted. While every effort has been made, it has not always been possible to identify the sources of all the material used, or to trace all copyright holders. If any omissions are brought to our notice, we will be happy to include the appropriate acknowledgements on reprinting.

p. 13: graphs and figures on tourism with permission from the Ministry of Tourism (New Zealand).

The authors and publishers would like to thank the following for permission to reproduce photographs:

Key: l = left, c = centre, r = right, t = top, b = bottom

Alamy/©UK Retail Alan King for p. 16 (l), /©Eric Nathan for p. 32, /©INSADCO Photography for p. 44, /©Neil Grant for p. 70; BP plc for p. 40 (1); Getty Images for p. 40 (3); ©Google Inc, 2007. Reprinted with permission for p. 40 (5); Masterfile/©Jon Feingersh for p. 11, /©Mike Randolph for p. 30 (b), /©WireImageStock for p. 52, /©Min Roman for p. 75; Photolibrary/©Imagestate Ltd for p. 14 (b); Punchstock/©Creatas for p. 10, /©Stockbyte for p. 41, /©image100 for p. 48 (l), /©Digital Vision for p. 48 (r), /©Polka Dot Images for p. 64, /©Digital Vision for p68 (l), /©Image Source for p. 68 (r), /©Stockbyte for p. 72; Rex for p. 40 (6); Sony Ltd for p. 40 (2); The Møller Centre, Cambridge for p. 36 (all); Toyota Motor Manufacturing Ltd for p. 40 (4); Wal-Mart Stores Inc. for p. 40 (7).

Many thanks also to The Møller Centre, residential management and conference centre in Cambridge for the use of the photos on page 36 and inspiration for Unit 7.

Illustrations:

Kathy Baxendale pp. 22, 37, 39, 60, 61; Mark Duffin pp. 14, 17b, 23, 26, 30, 33, 38, 45; Katie Mac pp. 18, 46, 66; Laura Martinez pp. 17t, 25, 28, 42, 59; Julian Mosedale pp. 12, 54; Ian West pp. 21, 51, 72

Text design and page make-up: Kamae Design, Oxford
Cover design: Kamae Design, Oxford
Cover photo: © Getty Images
Picture research: Hilary Luckcock

Introduction
To the student

Who is *Real Listening & Speaking 4* for?

You can use this book if you are a student at advanced level and you want to improve your English listening and speaking. You can use the book alone without a teacher or you can use it in a classroom with a teacher.

How will *Real Listening & Speaking 4* help me with my listening and speaking?

Real Listening & Speaking 4 contains practical tasks to help you in everyday listening and speaking situations, e.g. at the shops, sightseeing or travelling away from home. It also gives practice in a range of work and study situations. It is designed to help you with listening and speaking tasks you will need to do when communicating in English, at home or abroad.

The exercises in each unit help you to develop useful skills such as listening for context, listening for specific information and listening for the main idea. It is designed to help you with listening and speaking you will need to do when communicating in English at home or when visiting another country.

How is *Real Listening & Speaking 4* organized?

The book has 16 units and is divided into two main sections:
- Units 1–6 – social and travel situations
- Units 7–16 – work and study situations

Every unit has:
- *Get ready to listen and speak*: introduces you to the topic of the unit
- *Learning tip*: helps you improve your learning
- *Class bonus*: gives an exercise you can do with other students or friends
- *Speaking strategy*: explains a useful strategy
- *Speak up!*: practises the strategy
- *Extra practice*: gives an extra exercise for more practice
- *Can-do checklist*: helps you think about what you learnt in the unit

Most units also have:
- *Focus on*: helps you study useful grammar or vocabulary
- *Did you know?*: gives extra information about vocabulary, different cultures or the topic of the unit
- *Sound smart*: helps you with pronunciation

After each main section there is a review unit. The reviews help you practise the skills you learn in each section.

At the back of the book you can find:
- *Appendices*: contain lists of *Useful language* for every unit and more ideas about how to improve your listening and speaking
- *Audioscript*: includes everything that you can hear on the audio CDs and gives information about the nationalities of the speakers
- *Answer key*: gives correct answers and possible answers for exercises that have more than one answer

How can I use *Real Listening & Speaking 4*?

The book is in two sections: *Social and Travel*, and *Work and Study*. The units at the end of the book are more difficult than the units at the beginning of the book. However, you do not need to do the units in order. It is better to choose the units that are most interesting for you and to do them in the order you prefer.

There are many different ways you can use this book. We suggest you work in this way:
- Look in the *Contents* list and find a unit that interests you.
- Go to *Appendix 1* and look at the *Useful language* for the unit you want to do. You can use a dictionary to help you understand the words and expressions.
- Do the *Get ready to listen and speak* section at the start of the unit. This will introduce you to the topic of the unit.
- Do the other exercises in the unit. At the end of each exercise, check your answers in the *Answer key*.
- If your answers are wrong, study the section again to see where you made mistakes.
- Try to do the listening exercises without looking at the audioscript. You can read the audioscript after you finish the exercises. Some exercises ask you to respond to what you hear. You can pause the CD to give you time to say your answer.
- If you want to do more work in this unit, do the *Extra practice* activity.
- At the end of the unit, think about what you learnt and complete the *Can-do checklist*.
- Go to *Appendix 1* and look at the *Useful language* for the unit again.

Introduction

To the teacher

What is *Cambridge English Skills*?

Real Listening & Speaking 4 is one of 12 books in the *Cambridge English Skills* series. The series offers skills training to students from elementary to advanced level, and also contains *Real Reading* and *Real Writing* books. All the books are available in with-answers and without-answers editions.

Level	Book	Author
Elementary CEF: A2 Cambridge ESOL: KET NQF Skills for life: Entry 2	Real Reading 1 with answers	Liz Driscoll
	Real Reading 1 without answers	Liz Driscoll
	Real Writing 1 with answers and audio CD	Graham Palmer
	Real Writing 1 without answers	Graham Palmer
	Real Listening & Speaking 1 with answers and audio CDs (2)	Miles Craven
	Real Listening & Speaking 1 without answers	Miles Craven
Pre-intermediate CEF: B1 Cambridge ESOL: PET NQF Skills for life: Entry 3	Real Reading 2 with answers	Liz Driscoll
	Real Reading 2 without answers	Liz Driscoll
	Real Writing 2 with answers and audio CD	Graham Palmer
	Real Writing 2 without answers	Graham Palmer
	Real Listening & Speaking 2 with answers and audio CDs (2)	Sally Logan & Craig Thaine
	Real Listening & Speaking 2 without answers	Sally Logan & Craig Thaine
Intermediate to upper-intermediate CEF: B2 Cambridge ESOL: FCE NQF Skills for life: Level 1	Real Reading 3 with answers	Liz Driscoll
	Real Reading 3 without answers	Liz Driscoll
	Real Writing 3 with answers and audio CD	Roger Gower
	Real Writing 3 without answers	Roger Gower
	Real Listening & Speaking 3 with answers and audio CDs (2)	Miles Craven
	Real Listening & Speaking 3 without answers	Miles Craven
Advanced CEF: C1 Cambridge ESOL: CAE NQF Skills for life: Level 2	Real Reading 4 with answers	Liz Driscoll
	Real Reading 4 without answers	Liz Driscoll
	Real Writing 4 with answers and audio CD	Simon Haines
	Real Writing 4 without answers	Simon Haines
	Real Listening & Speaking 4 with answers and audio CDs (2)	**Miles Craven**
	Real Listening & Speaking 4 without answers	Miles Craven

Where are the teacher's notes?

The series is accompanied by a dedicated website containing detailed teaching notes and extension ideas for every unit of every book. Please visit www.cambridge.org/englishskills to access the *Cambridge English Skills* teacher's notes.

What are the main aims of *Real Listening & Speaking 4*?

- To help students develop listening and speaking skills in accordance with the ALTE (Association of Language Testers in Europe) Can-do statements. These statements describe what language users can typically do at different levels and in different contexts. Visit www.alte.org for further information.
- To encourage autonomous learning by focusing on learner training

What are the key features of *Real Listening & Speaking 4*?

- It is aimed at advanced learners of English at level C1 of the Council of Europe's CEFR (Common European Framework of Reference for Languages)
- It contains 16 four-page units, divided into two sections: *Social and Travel* and *Work and Study*
- *Listening & Speaking 4* units contain:
  - *Get ready to listen and speak* warm-up tasks to get students thinking about the topic
  - *Learning tips* which give students advice on how to improve their listening and their speaking
  - *Sound smart* activities which focus on pronunciation
  - *Focus on* activities which provide contextualized practice, in particular language or vocabulary areas
  - *Class bonus* communication activities for pairwork and group work so you can adapt the material to suit your classes
  - *Did you know?* boxes which provide notes on cultural or linguistic differences between English-speaking countries, or factual information on the topic of the unit
  - *Extra practice* extension tasks which provide more real-world listening and speaking practice
  - *Can-do checklist* in every unit to encourage students to think about what they have learnt
- There are two review units to practise skills that have been introduced in the units.
- It has an international feel and contains a range of native and non-native English accents.
- It can be used as self-study material, in class, or as supplementary homework material.
- It covers a wide range of highly practical activities that give students the skills they need to communicate effectively in everyday situations.

What is the best way to use *Real Listening & Speaking 4* in the classroom?

The book is designed so that there is no set way to work through the units. The units may be used in any order, although the more difficult units naturally appear near the end of the book, in the *Work and Study* section.

You can consult the unit-by-unit teacher's notes at www.cambridge.org/englishskills for detailed teaching ideas. However, as a general guide, different sections of the book can be approached in the following ways:

- *Useful language*: You can use the *Useful language* lists in the *Appendices* to preteach or revise the vocabulary from the unit you are working on.
- *Get ready to listen and speak*: It is a good idea to use this section as an introduction to the topic. Students can work on these exercises in pairs or groups. Some exercises require students to answer questions about their personal experience. These questions can be used as prompts for discussion. Some exercises contain a problem-solving element that students can work on together. Other exercises aim to clarify key vocabulary in the unit. You can present these vocabulary items directly to students.
- *Learning tips*: Focus on these and draw attention to them in an open class situation. An alternative approach is for you to create a series of discussion questions associated with the *Learning tip*. Students can discuss their ideas in pairs or small groups followed by open class feedback. The *Learning tip* acts as a reflective learning tool to help promote learner autonomy.
- *Class bonuses*: The material in these activities aims to provide freer practice. You can set these up carefully, then take the role of observer during the activity so that students carry out the task freely. You can make yourself available to help students or to analyze the language they produce during the activity.
- *Extra practice*: These tasks can be set as homework or out-of-class projects for your students. Alternatively, students can do some tasks in pairs during class time.
- *Can-do checklists*: Refer to these at the beginning of a lesson to explain to students what the lesson will cover, and again at the end so that students can evaluate their learning for themselves.
- *Appendices*: You may find it useful to refer your students to these.
- *Audioscripts*: occasionally non-native speaker spoken errors are included in the audio material. They are labelled *Did you notice?* in the audioscript and can be used in the classroom to focus on common errors.

Unit 1
How's it going?

go to Useful language p. 78

Get ready to listen and speak

● Do you …

	Yes	Sometimes	No
like going to parties?	☐	☐	☐
enjoy meeting new people?	☐	☐	☐
prefer to socialize only with people you know?	☐	☐	☐
hate making small talk with strangers?	☐	☐	☐
switch off if you are not interested in the conversation?	☐	☐	☐
prefer to listen to others than give your opinion?	☐	☐	☐

● What do you think your answers say about your character?

A Listening – Starting a conversation

1 🔘2 **Listen and complete these expressions you can use to start a conversation.**

a What _____did you get up_____ to at the weekend?
b How's _____ ?
c Did you _____ last night?
d It's _____ , hasn't it?
e So, how _____ ?
f Wow! I _____ .

2 🔘3 **Listen and match each response (1–6) with a conversation starter (a–f) in Exercise 1.**

1 _c_   2 _____   3 _____   4 _____   5 _____   6 _____

B Listening – Making small talk

1 🔘4 **Kerri, from Ireland, is at a party in a friend's home. Listen to two conversations (A and B) she has with people she meets. Circle the correct answer.**

Who …
a talks about himself?   Tim / Nick
b responds to information?   Tim / Nick
c doesn't ask questions?   Tim / Nick
d shows interest?   Tim / Nick
e asks lots of questions?   Tim / Nick

2 🔘4 **Which conversation is more successful? Why? Listen again and note your ideas.**

Learning tip

To get on well in conversation it's important to be a good listener. Listen carefully and respond to what you hear, showing interest and asking questions for more information. This will help keep the conversation going.

C Speaking – Keeping a conversation going (1)

Speaking strategy: Asking follow-up questions

1 **Look at this extract from Kerri's conversation with Nick. Underline the follow-up questions that Nick asks Kerri about her work.**

Kerri: We work in the same department.
Nick: Oh, I see. How long have you worked there?
Kerri: Nearly a year.
Nick: Great. Are you enjoying it?

Speak up!

2 **Imagine you are speaking to someone at a party. Write one follow-up question for each of these statements.**

a I've lived here for five years now.
 <u>Where did you live before?</u>

b I work in Manchester.
 ....

c I'm going on holiday soon.
 ....

d I went to Paris last week.
 ....

e I moved house last Monday.
 ....

3 ⏺️**5** **Now listen to eight statements (a–h). For each statement, respond by asking a follow-up question.**

Example
You hear: a
 I have two children.
You say: Oh really? What are their names?

D Speaking – Keeping a conversation going (2)

Speaking strategy: Using question tags

1 **Look at two more extracts from Kerri and Nick's conversation. How does Nick encourage Kerri to respond?**

a Nick: Great party, isn't it?
 Kerri: Yeah, it's really good.

b Kerri: Have you ever been to Dublin?
 Nick: No, but I've always wanted to go. It's not expensive, is it?

Notice that using a question tag turns a statement into a question and invites the listener to reply.

2 ⏺️**6** **Now listen to each extract. Does Nick's voice go up or down at the end of each question tag?**

a ...... b ......

3 **In which question …**

1 does Nick ask for clarification? ......
2 does he want Kerri to agree with him? ......

Speak up!

4 **Imagine you are speaking to someone at a party. Use the ideas below to make questions using question tags. Make your voice go down at the end, asking for agreement.**

Example: a John's a nice guy, isn't he?

a John / nice guy
b music / great
c cold / yesterday
d you / two children
e they / not from here
f your birthday / last week

5 **Now use the ideas below to make more questions using question tags. This time, make your voice go up at the end, asking for clarification.**

Example: a You don't live in London, do you?

a you / not live in London
b he / not find a job yet
c Julia / not pass driving test / last week
d you / not shopping / next weekend
e they / eat meat
f you / not watch the match / last night

E Speaking – Keeping a conversation going (3)

Speaking strategy: Reply questions

1 Look at another extract from Kerri's conversation with Nick. Notice how Nick shows interest by asking a short question *Do you?* This is called a *reply* question.

Kerri: I come from Dublin originally.
Nick: Do you? That's great. They say it's a really fun city.

Speak up!

2 Complete each conversation with a reply question.

a A: I bought a new car last month.
  B: _____Did you_____ ? What model did you go for?

b A: I don't like classical music at all.
  B: _____ ? I love it.

c A: I've got terrible backache.
  B: _____ ? Oh dear.

3 🄐7 Listen and check. Then play the recording again and take the role of B. Try to speak at the same time.

4 🄐8 Now listen to eight more statements and respond to each one with a reply question. Try to add a follow-up question too, if you can.

Example: You hear: a It's my birthday today.
You say: Is it? Congratulations. What are you going to do to celebrate?

Focus on ...
question tags

1 Make each statement a question by adding a question tag.
  a You haven't lived here long, ___have you___ ?
  b You like your job, _____ ?
  c Michael is a nice guy, _____ ?
  d Tina isn't coming for dinner tonight, _____ ?
  e I've seen you somewhere before, _____ ?
  f They come from Germany, _____ ?
  g You won't be late, _____ ?
  h We met at Julie's party last month, _____ ?

2 Say each question twice. First, make your voice go up, asking for clarification. Then make your voice go down, asking for agreement.

Did you know ...?

Conversations last longer when people smile and keep good eye contact.

Class bonus

Imagine you are at a party. Stand up, mingle with your classmates and start conversations together. Try to keep each conversation going as long as you can by asking follow-up questions, using question tags and reply questions. Use your body language to show interest and to relate to the people you are speaking to.

F Listening – Understanding irony

1 🄐9 Listen and complete conversations a and b.

a Emma: Oh no. It's _____ !
  Tony: Great. I was going to _____ this afternoon.

b Julie: It said on the news that _____ are going to fall.
  Frank: Really? That's great. I've just bought a _____ .

2 Look at each conversation again and tick ✓ your answers.

a How do Tony and Frank both feel?
  pleased ☐ relieved ☐ disappointed ☐ excited ☐
b When they say *Great / That's great,* what do they mean?
  'How wonderful!' ☐
  'Oh no. That's terrible!' ☐
  'I'm not interested.' ☐

3 🄐10 Now listen to three more conversations and match each conversation (a–c) to one of the pictures (1–3) below.

1 _____   2 _____

3 _____

4 🔟 **Listen again and match each expression you hear with a conversation.**

What a pity!	Conversation a
That's marvellous!	Conversation b
How exciting!	Conversation c

5 🔟 **Listen again. What does each speaker _really_ mean?**

a I'm pleased about that.
b How boring!
c What a disaster!

What a pity! _a_
That's marvellous! ......
How exciting! ......

Focus on ... ab🅒def
exclamations

Complete each exclamation with _How ...,_ _What ..._ or _What a ... ._

a __What__ a terrible thing to say!
b .... awful!
c .... pity!
d .... fantastic news!
e .... great idea!
f .... appalling weather!
g .... amazing!
h .... mess!
i .... unusual!
j .... relief!

Sound smart
Indicating emotion

1 🔟1️⃣ The _way_ you say something can change its meaning. Listen to these examples.

a Guess what? I've passed all my exams.   That's great. ↗

b There's nothing to do and nothing on TV either.   That's great. ↘

In the first example the speaker has a high tone and emphasizes _great_ to show enthusiasm. In the second example, the flat tone and lack of intonation on _great_ indicates boredom.

2 🔟1️⃣ Listen to the examples again and repeat each response.

3 1️⃣2️⃣ Now listen to each expression below spoken in a different way. Tick ✓ what emotion the speaker is trying to convey in each case.

	enthusiastic	bored
a That's really interesting.	✓	☐
b That's really interesting.	☐	☐
c How marvellous.	☐	☐
d How marvellous.	☐	☐
e That's exciting.	☐	☐
f That's exciting.	☐	☐
g What a good idea.	☐	☐
h What a good idea.	☐	☐

4 1️⃣2️⃣ Listen and check. Then listen again and repeat each sentence using the same intonation.

E🅧tra practice

Find an English-speaking club in your area. Go along with a friend to the next meeting. Use the question techniques and strategies in this unit to help you communicate with the people you meet there.

Can-do checklist

Tick what you can do.

	Can do	Need more practice
I can start up a conversation and make small talk.	✓	✓
I can keep a conversation going using a range of question techniques.		
I can understand when someone is being ironic.		
I can use intonation to indicate emotions such as enthusiasm.		

Unit 2
I'm looking for a camera

go to Useful language p. 78

Get ready to listen and speak

- Match each item (a–l) with a picture (1–12).
  - a DVD recorder _8_
  - b MP4 Player _____
  - c plasma TV _____
  - d desktop PC _____
  - e laptop/notebook computer _____
  - f smart phone _____
  - g USB memory stick _____
  - h digital camcorder _____
  - i all-in-one printer _____
  - j memory card _____
  - k SatNav system _____
  - l shredder _____

- Tick ✓ the items you own.

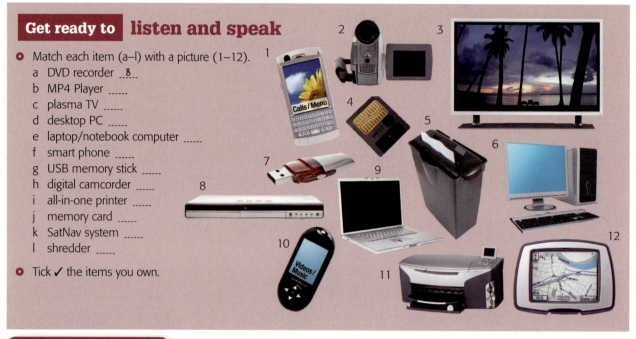

A Listening – In an electrical shop

1 🔊13 Listen to five short conversations in an electrical shop. For each conversation, decide which item (a–l) above the people are talking about.

- a SatNav system
- b _____
- c _____
- d _____
- e _____

2 🔊13 Listen again. Make a list of the words and expressions that help identify each item.

- a maps, plan your route, touch screen
- b _____
- c _____
- d _____
- e _____

B Listening – Asking for information

1 🔊14 Paola is an Italian teacher working in London. She's thinking of buying a smart phone. Listen to her talk to an assistant and complete the expressions she uses below.

- a I'm _____ looking for _____ a smart phone.
- b I'm _____ this one.
- c Can _____ wireless internet is?
- d Sorry, _____ 'hotspot' mean?
- e Could you _____ that?
- f I'd _____ more about that, please.
- g _____ the battery life _____ ?

2 Match each expression from Exercise 1 (a–g) with a function (1–3).

1 Asking for an explanation
   c ....

2 Asking for information
   ....

3 Saying what product you want
   ....

3 🔘**14** **Look at these things you can do with a smart phone. Listen again and number each one in the order it is mentioned (1–10).**

organize appointments ☐1
take notes and write documents ☐3
store addresses and contacts ☐2
surf the Internet ☐4
read and send email ☐9
listen to music ☐8
take photos and videos ☐6
watch TV ☐9
download video games ☐7
transfer files to your computer ☐

4 🔘**14** **Answer these questions, then listen once more and check.**

a What is the advantage of wireless internet? ....
....

b What is a 'hotspot'?
....
....

Did you know …?

WEEE means Waste Electrical and Electronic Equipment. Every year, millions of tonnes of old and unwanted electronic goods are thrown away. This creates a huge environmental problem. Governments, manufacturers and individuals around the world are trying to collect, reuse and recycle these unwanted electronic goods.

Sound smart
The schwa /ə/

The schwa is the weak vowel sound in some syllables that is pronounced /ə/. It is very common in spoken English.

1 🔘**15** Listen to these words. Notice the schwa.
connect   picture   computer

2 🔘**16** Now listen to these words. Underline the schwa in each word. It may appear more than once.
camera   popular   feature
address   appointment

3 🔘**17** Listen to this sentence. Notice the schwa.
I often use my phone to surf the Internet.

4 🔘**18** Now listen to these sentences. Underline the schwas.
a Can I take a closer look?
b Here's a picture of me and my friend.
c The assistant said there's a sale on today.

5 🔘**15–18** Listen again and repeat the words and sentences. Try to pronounce the schwa sound each time.

C Speaking – Finding out about a product

Speaking strategy: Asking how to use something

1 Look at this extract from the end of Paola's conversation. Notice the expression in bold that she uses to ask how to use the smart phone.

Paola: **What happens if I** press this button here?
Assistant: Er, nothing. You've got to turn it on first!

2 Here are some other expressions you can use to ask how something works.

What does that (button) **do**?
What is this (button) **for**?

Speak up!

3 🔘**19** **Imagine you want to buy a smart phone. Use the words below to make sentences. Listen and respond to the assistant.**

Example
You hear: Can I help you?
                    a
You say: Yes, please. I'm looking for a smart phone.

a look for / smart phone
b have / a closer look?
c happens / press this button?
d keypad / for?
e blue button / do?

D Listening – Making a purchase

1 🔘20 **James is buying a DVD recorder. Listen and tick ✓ which extra services the assistant mentions.**

Special payment terms ☑   An accessory at a reduced price ☐
An extended warranty ☑   Delivery ☑
After-sales technical support ☐   Installation and demonstration ☐

2 🔘20 **Listen again and write the cost of each additional service the assistant offers.**

----

3 🔘20 **Listen once more. Which service does James decide to buy? What does he *not* have to pay for?**

E Speaking – Getting a good deal

Speaking strategy: Negotiating

1 **Look at this extract from the conversation in the electrical shop. <u>Underline</u> the words James uses to bargain with the assistant.**

James: If you give me free delivery, then I'll take the extended warranty option. How's that?

Assistant: Hmm. OK. I think we can work something out here.

Speak up!

2 **Imagine you are a customer and want to bargain with the shop assistant. Use *If ... then* to negotiate these terms.**

Example: a free delivery / extended warranty
You say: If you give me free delivery, then I'll take the extended warranty.

a free delivery / extended warranty
b 10% off / special payment terms
c free installation and demonstration / extended warranty
d free delivery / after-sales technical support
e a discount / buy two
f give me an extra battery / buy the leather case

Focus on ...
the language of sales

Circle the correct preposition in each sentence.
a Are these printers *in* / *at* the sale?
b There's 25% *down* / *off* everything in the shop today.
c Have you got any special offers *on* / *in* at the moment?
d There's a sale *with* / *on* all plasma TVs this month.
e I'm sorry. That item is not *in* / *for* sale.
f All our computers are *in* / *on* the sale this week.
g We've had a bad month. Our sales are *down* / *under* by 10%.

Class bonus

Half the class are shop assistants, the other half are customers.
Shop assistants: Decide what electrical item you want to sell (e.g. a digital camcorder, plasma TV, notebook computer etc.). What is the full price? What extra services can you offer, and for how much?
Customers: Speak to various assistants. Find out what they are selling and decide what you want to buy. What extra services do you want? Try to negotiate a good deal.

F Listening – Returning an item to a shop

1 🔊 **21** Listen to four people each take an item back to a shop. Match each person with the item they are returning.

an all-in-one printer ....
a computer game ....
a mobile phone ....
an MP4 player ......_Jane_......

2 🔊 **21** Listen again and complete the reasons for returning each item.

Jane She never ......_listens to music._......
Henri He .... has ....
Pete It's faulty. The ....gets stuck and the .... doesn't work.
Karen It .... while on the Internet, and sometimes when she makes a call she
  can't ....

G Speaking – Returning items

Speaking strategy: Describing a problem

1 **Here are some expressions you can use to describe a problem.**

The thing is …
The problem is …
I don't understand why …
The problem seems to be …

2 🔊 **21** Listen again to Jane, Henri, Pete and Karen. Tick ✓ the expressions you hear.

> **E X tra practice**
>
> Imagine you are telling a friend about an electronic item you own. Say where you bought it, when, what features it has and if you have had any problems with it.

Speak up!

3 **Imagine you are a customer returning an item to a shop. Look at the information below and explain the problem to the shop assistant.**

Example: a
You say: I bought this radio last month but the problem is the volume doesn't work properly.

a bought last month / ~~volume~~

b bought last week / ~~screen~~

c present / ~~listen to music~~

d present / already have it

e bought last weekend / ~~remote control~~

Can-do checklist

Tick what you can do.

	Can do	Need more practice
I can ask about a range of products in detail.		
I can negotiate with a shop assistant to get a good deal.		
I can return an item and give an explanation where necessary.		

17

Unit 3
I need to see a doctor

● Match the health problems (a–f) with the symptoms (1–6).

a food poisoning 1 have a splitting headache, feel dizzy
b depression 2 have trouble sleeping, can't unwind or relax
c hay fever 3 have stomach cramps, feel nauseous, have diarrhoea
d migraine 4 feel lethargic, lacking in energy, pessimistic
e insomnia 5 have watery eyes, sneeze a lot, feel breathless
f a fever 6 have a high temperature, shiver and sweat

● What advice would you give someone suffering from these problems?

go to Useful language p. 79

A Listening – Getting the right healthcare

1 🎧22 **Listen and match each speaker (a–d) with a picture (1–4).**

2 🎧22 **Can you remember what each person wants? Note your answers, then listen again and check.**

a *something for a headache* _____
b _____
c _____
d _____

3 🎧23 **Now listen and match each reply (1–4) with the correct speaker (a–d) in Exercise 1.**

1 *d* 2 _____ 3 _____ 4 _____

4 🎧23 **Listen again to each reply and answer these questions.**

a What does MIU stand for?
_____
b How much do the headache tablets cost?
_____
c What does a new patient check-up involve?
_____
d What time is the doctor's appointment?
_____

B Listening – Registering at a doctor's surgery

1 🔘**24** **Beata is a student from Germany. She is registering at Cranfield House Surgery. Listen and complete the steps in the registration process.**

Step 1 fill in a .... form
Step 2 complete a .... card
Step 3 have a .... Check

2 🔘**24** **Listen again and answer the questions.**

a What documents does she need to provide?

----

b What additional information does she have to provide?

C Listening – Finding out about health services

1 🔘**25** **Listen to the receptionist tell Beata about the range of services offered at the medical practice. Number the services listed on the leaflet in the order she mentions them.**

Cranfield House Surgery

☐	Well Person Clinic	p1
☐	Asking for advice	p3
☐	Home visits	p4
☐	Seeing the nurse	p5
☐	Special clinics	p6
1	Making an appointment	p9
☐	Repeat prescriptions	p10
☐	In an emergency	p11

0131 732 8900

2 🔘**25** **Read the statements below. Then listen again and write T (true) or F (false) for each statement.**

a You can only make an appointment by phone. ..F..
b Usually you can see a doctor in less than 24 hours. ......
c Only a doctor can give vaccinations. ......
d You have to call before ten thirty if you want a home visit. ......
e A nurse or doctor is available seven days a week to give advice by phone. ......
f There is a Well Person Clinic twice a week. ......
g There is no special clinic for people with hay fever. ......
h You have to ask two days in advance for a repeat prescription. ......

3 **Now correct the false statements.**

Did you know …?

Citizens of many European countries are entitled to free or discounted medical treatment throughout Europe, with the European Health Insurance Card (EHIC). Citizens from outside the EU may have to pay for treatment if they become ill while visiting an EU country.

D Listening – At the doctor's

1 🔘 26 **Listen to two patients, Anne and Brian, describe their symptoms to the doctor. Write A (Anne) or B (Brian) next to each symptom below.**

1 can't switch off ⬛A⬛
2 is very lethargic ⬜
3 is shivering and sweating ⬜
4 has trouble sleeping ⬜
5 has a high temperature ⬜
6 feels tense and irritable ⬜
7 feels weak and dizzy ⬜

2 🔘 27 **What do you think could be the matter with each person? Listen to the doctor's diagnosis and complete his notes.**

Anne Bertrand

Problem: _depression_

Treatment: _Nitropan._ _–week course._
One 1000mg tablet _and another_

Return visit Yes/No [If yes, when _____]

Brian Kingston

Problem: _____

Treatment: _Cordosole 5. 1-week course._
250mg tablets, 3x per day before

Return visit Yes/No [If yes, when _____]

3 🔘 28 **A few weeks later Beata isn't feeling very well. She goes to see her doctor. Listen and tick ✓ the symptoms she mentions.**

has trouble sleeping ⬜
feels nauseous ✓
has stomach cramps ⬜ ✓
has diarrhoea ⬜ ✓
has been sick ⬜ ✓
has a high temperature ⬜

4 **Look at Beata's symptoms. What do you think is wrong with her?**

5 🔘 29 **Now listen to the doctor's diagnosis. Answer the questions.**

a What is wrong with Beata?

----

b What does the doctor prescribe?

----

c Does she have to go back to the doctor?

Learning tip

It is not always possible to understand everything first time. If you are not sure, then check you have understood, especially if the information is important. A good technique is to repeat the important information back to the speaker.

E Speaking – Understanding the diagnosis

Speaking strategy: Checking you understand

1 **Look at this extract from Beata's conversation with the doctor. How does she check she has understood correctly?**

Doctor: I'll give you a prescription for some tablets. They're very good. Take two every four hours and it should sort itself out in a few days.

Beata: OK, so I need to take two tablets every four hours.

2 **You can also use these expressions when you want to check you have understood.**

So, you mean I should …
Right, so you're saying I have to …

Speak up!

3 🔘 30 **Imagine you are at the doctor's. Listen to the doctor's instructions (a–e) and respond each time by checking you understand.**

Example
You hear: a
This is a prescription for some medicine that should help sort it out. Take two tablets three times a day, before meals.

You say: Right, so you're saying I have to take two tablets three times a day before meals.

Sound smart
Using stress to correct misunderstandings

1 🔘31 Stressing certain words is a useful way of correcting someone if they have misheard or misunderstood what you have said. Listen to these two conversations and notice how the words in **bold** have more stress.

A: So you have to take two tablets once a day?
B: No, the doctor said take two tablets **twice** a day.

A: Did you say your left ankle was swollen?
B: No, it's my **right** ankle.

2 🔘32 Now listen and use the information below to correct each speaker. Stress the important words in your reply.

Example
You hear: a
            So, your next appointment is on Friday at five thirty?
You say: No, it's on Friday at **six** thirty.

a Friday 6.30pm
b after each meal
c three times a day
d right arm
e a blood test

'So you're saying I have to take *three* of these?'
'That's right. Every four hours.'

E ✗ tra practice

Go to the BBC Learning English website and type 'health' in the search box. Press enter, then choose a link that interests you. Click 'Listen to the story' and check for any video material, too. Complete any exercises. You could also go to the Voice of America Special English website to watch or listen to more health stories.
http://www.bbc.co.uk/worldservice/learningenglish
http://www.voanews.com/specialenglish/

Class bonus

Half the class are doctors, the other half are patients.
Patients: Think of a health problem. Find a doctor and explain your symptoms. Then listen carefully to the doctor's diagnosis, and repeat back any instructions to make sure you understand. Visit several doctors to find who gives the best diagnosis and advice.
Doctors: Listen to each patient describe a health problem. Make a diagnosis and prescribe some medicine. Give instructions on taking the medicine. Make sure your patients understand clearly.

Can-do checklist

Tick what you can do.

	Can do	Need more practice
I can enquire effectively about and register for healthcare services.		
I can listen to a doctor's diagnosis and check I have understood.		
I can use stress to correct misunderstandings.		

Unit 4
What's the problem?

Get ready to listen and speak

- Label the diagrams using these words.
  pipe fuse screw switch plug
  thermostat screwdriver cable

- Match the expressions to complete six
  sentences.
  For example: A car engine can stall.

	car engine		run out of ink.
	battery		blow.
A	pump	can	stall.
	printer cartridge		go flat.
	computer		break.
	fuse		crash.

go to Useful language p. 79

A Listening – Dealing with everyday problems

1 **[33]** **Listen to these sounds. What do you think is happening? Try to complete the chart.**

	Object	Problem
a	car	
b		
c		

2 **[34]** **Now listen to the conversation (a–c) that follows each sound. Check that you correctly identified each problem.**

3 **[34]** **Listen again. What does each person decide to do?**

a ....

b ....

c ....

Learning tip

It can sometimes be useful to listen not only to what people say, but also to any sounds in the background. You can find out a lot of information by listening for aural clues.

Focus on ...
modals of deduction

When we think we are sure about something we use *must* and *can't*.
It *must* be the battery.
No. It *can't* be. It's new. The fuse *must* have blown.

When we are not sure about something we use *may*, *might* or *could*.
It *may* be the battery.
Yeah, or it *might* be the fuse.
Hmm. It *could* have run out of paper, too.

1 Study the examples above and listen again to the conversations in Recording 34. Then circle the correct answers to complete the rules.
To make a deduction in the *present / past*, we use a modal of deduction and the infinitive.
To make a deduction in the *present / past*, we use a modal of deduction + *have* + past participle.

2 Now circle the correct answer to complete each sentence.
a It *might / can't* need a new fuse because I replaced it yesterday.
b There's no cable! Someone *must have / could have* taken it.
c This page is blank. I'm not sure, but the printer *could have / must have* run out of ink.
d The remote control isn't working. The batteries *might have / can't have* run out.
e The TV works fine now. I suppose someone *might have / must have* fixed it.
f The garage *might not / could not* be open. It's nearly six o'clock.

B Speaking – Finding solutions

Speaking strategy: Speculating about causes

1 **Look at these expressions you can use to speculate about causes. Notice the words in bold.**

The battery **may** be dead.
It **might have** run out of paper.
It **could** be the cable.
It **can't** be the fuse.
The cartridge **must have** run out.
Perhaps it **needs** replacing.

Speak up!

2 🔵35 **Imagine you are living with a friend. Your friend tells you about some problems around the home. Listen and use the ideas below to speculate about possible causes.**

Example
You hear: a
          Guess what? The dishwasher isn't working again.
You say: It could be the pump. It might have broken.
          Perhaps it needs replacing.

3 🔵36 **Now imagine your computer isn't working. Your friend suggests some possible causes. Listen and use the ideas below to have a conversation.**

Example
You hear: Is there something wrong with your computer? It
          could be the cable. It might not be plugged in.
          a
You say: No, I've checked all the cables. It can't be
          the cables.

a cables OK
b fuses OK
c monitor OK
d wireless keyboard and mouse – new batteries
e hard disk – not checked

a pump broken? / replace?

b batteries flat? / replace?

c cartridge run out?

d thermostat broken?

e fuse blown? / buy a new fuse?

C Speaking – Offering your opinion

Speaking strategy: Giving strong advice

1 Underline the expressions for giving strong advice.

You really should get this fixed.
You really shouldn't leave it any longer.
You'd better call an electrician.
You'd better not touch that cable. It might not be safe.
You ought to call a plumber.

Did you know …?

The negative of *ought to* is *ought not to* or *oughtn't to*. However, these negative forms are not common in spoken English.

Speak up!

2 🔊37 Listen to five people tell you about a problem. Use the ideas below to respond giving strong advice.

Example
You hear: a
          The toilet doesn't flush properly. I think I'll take a look.
You say: You ought to call a plumber. You shouldn't try to fix it yourself.

a call a plumber ✓ / fix it yourself ✗
b call an electrician ✓ / touch that cable ✗
c read the instructions again ✓ / take it back yet ✗
d call an engineer ✓ / take a look yourself ✗
e see a doctor ✓ / wait and to see if it gets better ✗

3 🔊38 Now imagine a friend has a problem with his car. Listen and use the ideas below to have a conversation.

Example
You hear: My car isn't running properly again. I'm a bit worried about it.
          a
You say: You'd better not drive it. You really should take it to a garage or it might break down.

a drive it ✗ / take to a garage ✓ / break down?
b leave it ✗ / get worse ?
c repair it yourself ✗ / mechanic ✓
d use car ✗ / train ✓
e buy ticket in advance ✓ / busy tomorrow a.m. ?

D Speaking – Speculating about consequences

Speaking strategy: Explaining consequences

1 Here are some expressions you can use to explain consequences. Underline the consequence in each sentence.

If you have a burglar alarm fitted, **then** this will act as a deterrent.
You will be ill **unless** you eat more healthily.
You should be more careful, **otherwise** you will have an accident.

Speak up!

2 🔊39 Listen and respond to each statement you hear using the ideas below and *if … then*, *unless* or *otherwise*.

Example
You hear: a
          I've got a really bad toothache.
You say: You should go to the dentist, otherwise it'll get worse.

a go to the dentist / get worse
b work hard / fail exams
c eat more healthily / put on weight
d get it repaired / fall behind with work
e apologize / lose your job

E Listening – Coping in an emergency

1 (40) **Listen and match each emergency (a–d) with a picture (1–4).**

a ..3..   b ....   c ....   d ....

1

2

3

4

2 (40) **Listen again and find one mistake in each of the pictures (1–4) above.**

1 ....   3 ....

2 ....   4 ....

3 (41) **Now listen to each person explain what they did. Write the name of each person next to the correct explanation (1–4).**

1 ...Jane...   2 ....   3 ....   4 ....

4 (41) **Listen again. Would you have done the same?** ....

Did you know …?

Many people store an ICE number on their mobile phone. ICE stands for **I**n **C**ase of **E**mergency. It is the number of a friend or relative that can be called in an emergency.

Class bonus

With your partner, think of a different emergency situation. Include as many details as you can, and then decide what you would do. When you are ready, describe your emergency situation to the class.

E**X**tra practice

Go to this link and choose a video to watch that interests you.
http://www.videojug.com/tag/first-aid

Can-do checklist

Tick what you can do.

	Can do	Need more practice
I can describe everyday problems and speculate about their causes.		
I can give advice and make strong recommendations.		
I can explain the consequences of particular actions.		

Unit 5
What a lot of red tape!

○ Look at the pictures and identify the documents. Which of these documents do you have?

○ Have you ever needed to get a permit or visa?

go to Useful language p. 79

A Listening – Contacting the visa office

1 🔵42 Imagine you are on holiday in the UK. You call the UK Visa section to find out what visa you require to study there. Listen to this recorded announcement. Which number should you press to continue your enquiry? ....

2 🔵43 Now listen to the next part of the message. Take notes of all the important information.

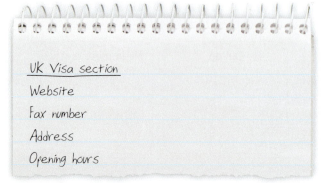

UK Visa section

Website

Fax number

Address

Opening hours

Did you know …?

'Red tape' describes official rules and processes. It is often used in a negative way, when these processes seem time-consuming and unnecessary, e.g. *My visa application took ages because there was so much red tape.*

Learning tip

When you take notes, note only the key words. Listen closely for any numbers, times, dates, names and addresses. Use abbreviations and symbols wherever possible. You can use your own abbreviations as well as standard ones.

B Listening – Enquiring about a visa

1 🔘44 Yuki, from Japan, is on holiday in England. She phones the UK Visa section to ask about getting a Student Visa for the UK. Number her questions (a–f) in the order you hear them (1–6).

a Can I work if I have a Student Visa? ☐
b How much is it? ☐
c What do I need to do to get a visa? ☐
d Can you tell me if I need a visa? ☐ 1
e What do you mean by 'supporting documents'? ☐
f How do I apply? ☐

2 🔘44 Now listen again and note the answer to each question.

1 Yes, she needs a visa.
2 ....
3 ....
4 ....
5 ....
6 ....

C Speaking – Making sure you understand

Speaking strategy: Asking for clarification

1 Look at this extract from the conversation between Yuki and the visa officer. Underline the expression she uses to ask the visa officer to explain a term she doesn't understand.

Visa officer: … with your passport, two recent colour passport-sized photos and the necessary supporting documents.

Yuki: Sorry, what do you mean by 'supporting documents'?

2 Here are some other expressions you can use.

What exactly does … mean?
I'm sorry. Can you explain what … means?
Sorry. I don't understand. What are …?

Speak up!

3 🔘45 Imagine you are speaking to a UK visa official. Listen to each statement and use the expressions above to ask for clarification. Then listen to the answer.

Example
You hear: You'll need entry clearance to come to the UK.
          a
You say: What exactly does 'entry clearance' mean?
You hear: Entry clearance means official permission to enter the country, so a visa or entry clearance certificate.

a entry clearance?
b IAS?
c UK Mission?
d the Schengen area?
e an EEA country?

Focus on … official language

Imagine you are applying for a visa. Here are some phrases you may hear. Complete each sentence with a word or phrase from the box.

status	run out	signature	print
register	~~official~~	fill in	origin

a The ____official____ dealing with your application is at counter 17.
b Please _____ this form and take a ticket.
c Your passport will _____ in a few months. You need to renew it.
d If you want to make an application then you have to _____ first.
e We need your _____ at the bottom of every page.
f Can you _____ your name in block capitals please?
g What's your marital _____ ?
h Please put your name and country of _____ .

D Listening – Applying for a green card in the US

1 🔊 46 **Listen to this US immigration official talk about how to get permanent residency in the US. What are the three main ways you can get a green card?**

	Ways of obtaining a green card	Requirements
1		
2		
3		

2 🔊 46 **Now listen again and note the requirements for each type of green card application.**

3 🔊 47 **Read the requirements. Then listen and number each requirement (a–e) in order (1–5).**

a Your US employer must file Form ETA 750. ☐ 1
b Your employer must send in Form I-140. ☐ 4
c The Department of State must approve your Immigrant Visa Petition. ☐ 3
d The Department of Labor must approve the request. ☐ 2
e You are given an Immigrant Visa Number. ☐ 5

4 🔊 48 **Look at the list below. Listen and tick which things are also needed in order to get permanent residency in the US.**

birth certificate ☐
driving licence ☐
ID Card ☐
biographical information ☐
passport ☐
two colour photos ☐

fingerprints ☐
a physical ☐
an interview ☐
marriage certificate ☐
a work permit ☐
a letter from your employer ☐

Did you know …?

A green card is not actually green in colour! It gives a non-US citizen permanent resident status in the US. This gives them the same rights as a US citizen, and means they can live, work and study there legally. In some states they can even vote in elections.

E Speaking – Giving explanations

Speaking strategy: Being concise and to the point

1 If you have an interview for a visa or permit, you will need to answer questions that the officials may have regarding your application. Should you …

a keep your answers short and to the point?
b talk a lot, giving all the information you can think of?

Speak up!

2 🔘 49 Read situations 1 and 2 below. For each situation, imagine you are having an interview with an immigration official. Listen to five questions and answer each one as clearly and precisely as you can.

Example
You hear: So, when did you arrive in France? a
You say: Three weeks ago.

1 You are travelling through Europe on holiday. You've been in France for three weeks and really like it. You want to stay longer so you have found a job in a supermarket. You need to apply for a temporary work permit. You intend to leave in a few months to continue your trip around Europe. You have all the necessary supporting documentation.

2 You are studying sociology at university in Canada. You need to get a job to support yourself for the next year while you study. You have found a job in a local restaurant but you need a work permit to work off campus. You haven't got a Social Insurance Number.

Class bonus

1 Prepare to role play an interview for a visa. Decide with your partner who will be the interviewer and who will be the applicant.

Interviewer: Make a list of questions to ask. You can use the questions in this unit to help you.

Applicant: Prepare for the interview. Anticipate what questions you may be asked and practise your answers. Use the guidance in this unit to help you.

2 Now role play the interview. When you finish, swap roles.

E ✗tra practice

Imagine an English-speaking friend wants to work in your country. Go on the Internet and find out how to apply for a work permit. Make notes, then imagine you are explaining this to your friend. Talk about what they need to do. If possible, record what you say and listen to yourself afterwards. Can you identify any areas you could improve, e.g. grammar, pronunciation, etc.?

Can-do checklist

Tick what you can do.

	Can do	Need more practice
I can enquire about official procedures, e.g. how to apply for a visa.		
I can understand explanations of the various steps involved in official processes.		
I can answer questions clearly and concisely.		

Unit6
What a great view!

Get ready to listen and speak

- Look at the pictures and identify the things you might see on a sightseeing holiday in a city.

- Tick ✓ the things you try to see when you look around a city.

- What other things do you like to see or do on a city break?

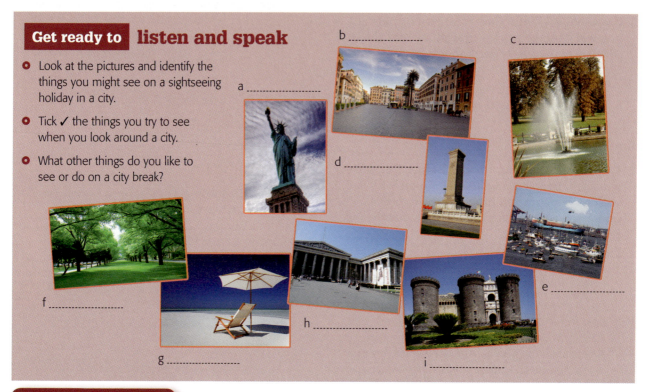

a _____

b _____

c _____

d _____

e _____

f _____

g _____

h _____

i _____

go to Useful language p. 79

A Listening – Showing someone around

1 🎧50 **Listen to Sarah show her friend Paul around her home town. What do you think each of these places is?**

Ronelles	a nightclub
Crosswell Hill	_____
Old Keller	_____
The Typewriter	_____
Figo's	_____

2 🎧50 **Listen again. Make a list of the words and expressions that helped you decide what each place is.**

Ronelles	lights outside, dancing, clubbing
Crosswell Hill	_____
Old Keller	_____
The Typewriter	_____
Figo's	_____

Learning tip

Listening for context is a useful skill. Listen out for key words and try to identify a common theme, e.g. if you hear *huge, made of marble,* and *an important person* then this might be a *statue.*

Focus on ...
strong adjectives

1 Match each adjective in A with a stronger adjective in B.

Example: big – huge

A	B
tired	furious
bad	huge
interesting	starving
angry	fantastic
big	terrible
scared	fascinating
hungry	tiny
good	terrified
small	exhausted

2 Circle the correct word to complete the rules.
You can make the adjectives in A stronger by adding *very / absolutely*.
You can make the adjectives in B stronger by adding *very / absolutely*.

3 Complete each sentence with *very* or *absolutely* and an adjective.
a The talk wasn't fantastic but it was ___very good___ .
b I wasn't scared. I was _____ .
c Everyone felt tired but Jim was _____ .
d Tina wasn't furious, but she was _____ .
e I wouldn't say the film was terrible, but it was
_____ .
f I'm not _____ but I am hungry.

Sound smart
Exaggerating

1 🔊51 Listen to this extract from Sarah and Paul's conversation. Notice how Paul emphasizes *starving* to express how hungry he is.
Sarah: Yeah. It's famous for its sandwiches. They're the best in town.
Paul: Great. I'm starving!

2 🔊52 Look at the statements below and listen. Notice how the stress and intonation help to emphasize the emotion.

I'm starving!	We're exhausted!
It's fantastic!	It's huge!
How terrible!	That's fascinating!
I'm furious!	I was terrified!

3 🔊53 Now listen and use the ideas below to reply to each statement in an exaggerated way.

Example
You hear: a
           Are you hungry?
You say: Yes, I am. I'm starving!
a starving!
b exhausted!
c fantastic!
d tiny!
e terrible!
f fascinating!
g furious!
h huge!

B Speaking – Talking about places of interest

Speaking strategy: Describing features

1 🔊50 Look at these expressions you can use to talk about places of interest. Listen again to the conversation between Sarah and Paul. Tick ✓ the expressions they use.

It's a good place to go if …
It's handy for … / It's popular for …
It's famous for … /   You can find/see … there.

Speak up!

2 Think about your home town. Make a list of places you know, and note what people can do there.

Places to go in my home town
Chicago's restaurant - great pizza

3 Now imagine you are showing a friend around your home town. Use your notes, and the expressions in Exercise 1, to talk about places of interest.

Example: Chicago's is a good place
to go if you like pizza.

4 Record yourself while you are speaking, then listen to the recording and evaluate your performance. Can you identify any areas to improve, e.g. grammar, pronunciation, etc?

C Listening – Asking about attractions

1 🔊 **54** **Mark is speaking to a travel agent about his next holiday. Listen and complete each question he asks.**

a Is it easy _____to get to_____ ?
b How _____ is it, once you're there?
c What's it like to _____ ?
d _____ to do?
e Are there any _____ ?
f What's the _____ ?
g What's the _____ like?
h Is it _____ anything in particular?
i Are there any _____ nearby?
j When's the _____ to go?

🔊 **54** Listen again and repeat each question.

2 🔊 **55** **Now listen to the travel agent's answers. Match each answer (1–10) with the correct question (a–j).**

1 _b_   2 _____   3 _____   4 _____   5 _____
6 _____   7 _____   8 _____   9 _____   10 _____

3 🔊 **55** **Look at the statements below. Write T (true) or F (false) for each statement, then listen again and check your answers.**

a Accommodation is reasonable, even in the centre. _F_
b It's a good place to go if you like different types of cuisine. _____
c It's best to hire a car if you want to see everything. _____
d There isn't anywhere interesting to go nearby. _____
e It's a good place for relaxing on the beach. _____
f The weather isn't usually very hot. _____
g It's easy to get around the city using public transport. _____
h It's very popular for people who like nightclubs and dancing. _____

4 Can you guess which famous US city this is?

_____

D Speaking – Giving advice on where to go

Speaking strategy: Making strong recommendations

1 Look at the statements below and notice the expressions you can use to make strong recommendations.

You **really ought to** see the castle.
You **should definitely** go in summer.
The museum is **well worth** a visit.
You certainly **mustn't** miss the park.
You **have to** see the main square in the evening.

2 🔊 55 Listen again to the travel agent's answers to Mark's questions. Tick ✓ each time the travel agent uses each expression.

Speak up!

3 Use the ideas below to make strong recommendations and add a reason.

Example: a
You say: You really ought to see the museum. It's absolutely fantastic!

a fantastic   b fascinating   c wonderful   d huge   e beautiful

4 Imagine a friend is visiting a city you know well. Look at the topics below and use the expressions above to make some recommendations.

Example: a
You say: You should definitely stay at The Grand Hotel. It's the best in town.

a where to stay   b getting around   c what to see and do
d places to eat   e nightlife   f the best time to go

Can-do checklist

Tick what you can do.

	Can do	Need more practice
I can show someone around my home town.		
I can describe places of interest.		
I can enquire about a city and ask about its main attractions.		
I can make strong recommendations about places of interest.		

Review 1
Units 1–6

Section 1

 58 Listen and reply to each statement you hear. (Circle) your answer.

1
a It's great, but the thing is, it doesn't fit.
b I'm very interested in this sweater.
c It's a great sweater, isn't it?

2
a Not at the moment, thank you.
b Yes, they are.
c Thanks very much.

3
a Isn't it?
b What a mess!
c Is it?

4
a You'd better get it serviced.
b It can't be anything else.
c The garage must have fixed it.

5
a No, it's not.
b You do, don't you?
c Do you? That's interesting.

6
a Yes, I am, aren't I?
b Yes, I am. I'm exhausted!
c Am I?

7
a Yes, you should definitely be.
b I agree completely.
c Can you explain what 'eligible' means?

8
a It might have run out.
b It could be the cable.
c The pump might need replacing.

9
a Aren't you?
b Don't you?
c Won't you?

10
a Yes, you really ought to.
b You should definitely stay at the Grand.
c No, I'd much rather you didn't.

Section 2

59 Read each situation. Then listen and tick ✓ the best reply.

1 You're buying a mobile phone in a shop. The assistant is trying to sell you an extended warranty. What do you say?

a ☐   b ☐   c ☐

2 Your friend tells you that their watch isn't working. What do you say?

a ☐   b ☐   c ☐

3 Your friend asks about the town where you grew up. What do you say?

a ☐   b ☐   c ☐

4 Your friend tells you their washing machine has broken. What do you say?

a ☐   b ☐   c ☐

5 A government official tells you that you need to fill out a Statutory Waiver Form. What do you say?

a ☐   b ☐   c ☐

6 The shredder you bought last month has broken. You take it back to the shop. What do you say?

a ☐   b ☐   c ☐

7 You are visiting a town for the first time when a tourist asks you for advice on what to see. What do you say?

a ☐   b ☐   c ☐

8 You are trying to get a good deal in a shop. What do you say?

a ☐   b ☐   c ☐

9 A friend tells you they are going to try to repair their television. What do you say?

a ☐   b ☐   c ☐

10 You are thinking of buying a smart phone, but don't know much about them. What do you say to the assistant?

a ☐   b ☐   c ☐

Section 3

Read each situation and circle your answer.

1 Your doctor is explaining how to take some medicine, but you are not sure you have understood correctly. What do you do?
   a Look confused and hope the doctor will repeat.
   b Repeat the instructions to the doctor.
   c Say nothing and decide to phone later.

2 What should you do if a customs official asks you questions at an airport?
   a Pretend you don't understand.
   b Keep your answers short and to the point.
   c Give as much information as you can think of.

3 Which of these expressions can you use to ask for information in a shop?
   a I'd like to know more about …
   b You really ought to tell me more about …
   c Right, so you're saying I have to find out more about …

4 To show approval, should your voice …
   a go down at the end of the sentence?
   b go up at the end of the sentence?
   c stay at the same level?

5 You think it's 6 o'clock, but you aren't sure. What is the best way to ask?
   a Say 'It's six o'clock, isn't it?' making your voice go down at the end.
   b Say 'It isn't six o'clock, is it?' with no change in intonation.
   c Say 'It's six o'clock, isn't it?' making your voice go up at the end.

6 Which of these things should you *not* do when you take notes?
   a Note only the key words.
   b Use abbreviations.
   c Try to write everything you hear.

7 Your friend looks very ill. What do you say?
   a You really should see a doctor.
   b If you see a doctor, I'll see one too.
   c You'd better not see a doctor.

8 To help prepare for a conversation, what should you *not* do?
   a Take a large dictionary with you, to look up words you don't know.
   b Make a list of any questions you want to ask.
   c Think about what you want to say and how to say it.

9 Which of these is *not* a good way to keep a conversation going?
   a Ask lots of follow-up questions.
   b Give short answers.
   c Use question tags.

10 If a shop assistant tells you a mobile phone has 'wireless internet', but you don't understand what it means, what should you say?
   a Have you got a dictionary?
   b Can I take a closer look?
   c Can you explain what 'wireless internet' is, please?

Section 4

Read each statement and write your reply.

1 I worked all weekend.

   ----

2 I have an exam next week and I haven't done any revision yet.

   ----

3 Good news. You've just won £100,000!

   ----

4 What's wrong with this DVD recorder? It won't work?

   ----

5 I've got three children, you know.

   ----

6 What did you think of the lecture?

   ----

7 Where are the best places to visit in your home town?

   ----

8 Great party, isn't it?

   ----

9 You need to send all these documents to the INS.

   ----

10 I have very bad toothache.

Unit 7
I'd appreciate it

Get ready to listen and speak

- Look at this brochure for a conference and training centre in Cambridge, UK. Match each statement (a–h) with a picture (1–4).

a   all rooms en-suite   ......

b   impressive modern building   ......

c   complimentary toiletries   ......

d   varied dishes, including full vegetarian option   ......

e   large and small meeting rooms available   ......

f   video conferencing capability   ......

g   inspired, international cuisine   ......

h   light, spacious meeting rooms   ......

go to Useful language p. 80

A Listening – Understanding detailed requirements

1   Mark is the sales manager at The Møller Centre. Listen as he takes a call from a client asking about organizing a conference there. Answer the questions.

a   What event does the client want to hold?
    <u>annual sales conference</u>

b   How many days will it last? _____

c   Has the client used The Møller Centre before? _____

d   Which of these items are provided at no extra charge?

a whiteboard ☐   a flipchart ☐

delegate pads/pencils ☐   water ☐

newspapers ☐   wireless Internet access ☐

> ### Learning tip
>
> If possible, try to identify the information you need before you listen. Make sure you know exactly what you are listening for, then try to focus only on those key details while you listen. Ignore everything else and don't worry if you don't understand everything.

2 🔁 **Now listen again and complete the booking sheet.**

Conference booking sheet

The Møller Centre

| Company: | ARG |
| Key contact: | Natasha Peters |

Conference details

Dates:

Number of people:

Accommodation

| Single rooms: 32 | Double rooms: |

Requests/Special requirements:

Training

Study Centre ☐ Shelley ☐ Byron ☐ Keats
☐ Wordsworth ☐ Browning

Meeting Room ☐ A ☐ B ☐ C ☐ D ☐ E ☐ F

Additional Equipment:

Catering

☐ Full-board ☐ Half-board

| Refreshment breaks: | | |
| Times | am | pm |

Additional information:

B Speaking – Asking for services

Speaking strategy: Making polite requests

1 🔁 **Look at these expressions you can use to ask for goods or services. Listen again to Mark's conversation with the client. Tick ✓ the expressions you hear the client use to make a polite request.**

Would you mind …ing?   I'd appreciate it if you could …
Could you possibly …?   I wonder if you could …
Can I ask you to …?   I'd be grateful if you could …

Speak up!

2 **Imagine you are organizing a conference for your company. You call the conference centre to make some final changes. Use the ideas below to make polite requests.**

Example: a
You say: I'd appreciate it if you could give us three
          rooms with a bath, rather than a shower.

a   three rooms with bath (not shower)
b   all rooms on ground floor
c   refreshment breaks – 3 pm not 3.30 pm
d   fresh flowers (all rooms)
e   early morning call 7 am (all rooms/every day)

3 **Now imagine that during the conference you need to make some more requests. Use the information below.**

Example: a
You say: Mr Hammond wants to move from the ground
          floor to the top floor. Would you mind checking
          to see if that's possible?

a   Mr Hammond ground floor → top floor

b turn up (all rooms)

c repair (Room G29)

d lend (tomorrow morning, Meeting Room C)

e   all training rooms

C Speaking – Overcoming language difficulties

Speaking strategy: Explaining what you want

1 <u>Underline</u> the expressions you can use to explain what you want when you don't know the word in English.

a I don't know what it's called but you use it to clean your teeth.

b I need something to put these posters on a display board.

c Have you got anything for cleaning marks off clothes?

2 🔵3 **Match each statement (a–c) above with a response (1–3). Then listen and check.**

1 Sure. Here are some drawing pins.

2 Yes, of course. I'll get you some stain remover.

3 A toothbrush? Yes, you can buy one at reception.

D Listening – Specifying your requirements

1 🔵5 **Peter works for a shipping company in Dubai. Listen to him speak to his boss, Viktor. Tick ✓ the adjective that you think best describe Viktor's attitude.**

cooperative ☐ angry ☐ bored ☐
reluctant ☐ friendly ☐

2 🔵5 **Listen again and answer the questions.**

a What project is Peter working on at the moment?

----

b Why does he say he needs some help?

----

c What help does he ask for? -----------------------

d How does he justify this request? -----------------

e When is the deadline? ------------------------------

f What help does Viktor agree to provide?

Did you know …?

Dubai is known as the 'Pearl of the Arabian Gulf'. It is a worldwide business hub, with over 170 shipping companies operating into and out of the emirate. As well as its excellent location, companies and individuals do not have to pay tax in Dubai!

Speak up!

3 🔵4 **Imagine you are at a conference venue. You need to use the items below (a–d) but you don't know the name in English. Use the expressions in Exercise 1 to explain what you need to the receptionist. Then listen to the answers.**

Example
You hear: Hello. Can I help you? a
You say: I need something to make holes in paper so I can put it in a file.
You hear: No problem. You can use this hole punch.

Sound smart
Detecting mood

1 🔵6 Listen to the same sentence spoken in four different ways. Match each sentence (a–c) with the speaker's attitude.

a OK, I'll do it for you now. — friendly/cooperative
b OK, I'll do it for you now. — angry/impatient
c OK, I'll do it for you now. bored/uninterested

2 🔵6 Listen again. Notice how the speaker's voice changes to reflect their mood.

3 🔵7 Now listen to eight more sentences. How does each speaker sound? Write the number of each sentence (1–8) next to the way each speaker feels.
friendly/cooperative ☐ ☐
angry/impatient ☐1☐ ☐
bored/uninterested ☐ ☐ ☐ ☐

E Speaking – Arguing your case

Speaking strategy: Asking for something and justifying reasons

1 Look at the sentences below. Notice the expressions in **bold** that you can use to ask for something and justify your reasons.

I could (really) do with a hand.
It would help a lot if someone could write up the report.
I'm in danger of falling behind.
I may not finish on time **if I don't** get any help.

2 🔵5 Listen again to the conversation between Peter and Viktor. Tick ✓ the expressions in Exercise 1 you hear.

Speak up!

3 Imagine you work in an office. Use the ideas below to make requests, and justify your reasons.

Example: a
You say: I could really do with some help to finish this
    sales report. I'm in danger of missing the deadline.

a help to finish (miss deadline)

b explain how to use (make mistakes)

c need new, colour printer (reports not clear)

d help photocopy reports (not finish in time)

e need holiday soon (become ill)

Focus on ... interrupting

1 Look at this extract from Peter's conversation with Viktor. Notice what Peter says to interrupt Viktor.
Peter: Oh, sorry Viktor. Are you in the middle of something?

2 Match the phrases to make complete statements.
  1 Are you   a disturb you.
  2 Am I   b anything, am I?
  3 I'm not interrupting c got a minute?
  4 Have you   d come back later if you like.
  5 Sorry to   e in the middle of something?
  6 I can   f interrupting?

Class bonus

1 Imagine you and your partner both work together in an office. Prepare to role play the following situation.

  A   B
  Interrupt politely
                             Ask how you can help
  Explain a problem
                             Express sympathy
  Make a request
                             Respond negatively
  Justify your request
                             Respond positively

2 Now role play the conversation.

E✗tra practice

Go to the BBC *Learning English* website and type 'making requests' in the search box. Press enter, then choose a link that interests you. Complete any exercises.
http://www.bbc.co.uk/worldservice/learningenglish

Can-do checklist

Tick what you can do.

	Can do	Need more practice
I can understand detailed requirements.		
I can make polite requests and explain what I want.		
I can interrupt politely and ask for help.		
I can specify my requirements and justify my reasons.		

Unit 8
This is your office

Get ready to listen and speak

- What do you know about these international companies? Match each company (1–7) with its area of business activity (a–g).
  - a oil and gas exploration ......
  - b banking and finance ......
  - c automotive manufacturing ......
  - d retail ......
  - e computer technology ......
  - f Internet search and advertising ......
  - g electronics manufacturing ......

- In your view, is it better to work for a large or a small company?

go to Useful language p. 80

Did you know …?

Google came top of Fortune magazine's '100 Best Companies to Work For'. The company receives over 1,300 curriculum vitaes (CVs) every day.

A Listening – Getting an overview

1 🔘 **18** Colin Vickerstaff is a company director. He is speaking to a group of new graduate trainees. Listen and complete the company profile.

2 🔘 **19** Now listen as Colin outlines the company's Mission Statement. Which slogan (a–d) best describes the values of the company?

   a Committed to continuous improvement
   b Quality, Price and Speed
   c The Customer is King
   d Investment in People

3 🔘 **10** Listen as Colin describes the management organization of his company. Complete the chart.

Company profile

Name: AGM Industries _____
Established: _____
Main activity: _____
Headquarters: _____
Turnover: _____
No. of employees: _____
Current market share: _____

Learning tip

When listening for the main idea, focus on the overall message rather than individual words and phrases. Take a mental 'step back' and try not to be distracted by small details.

a Chairman

b _____   CEO

| Operations | Technical Services | Business Development | Finance | Strategy and Planning | c _____ | Customer Services |

Product Management   d _____   Quality Control   e _____   f _____

B Speaking – Talking about organizations

Speaking strategy: Describing a company

1 Study the language below that you can use to describe a company and its activities. Notice the words and expressions in **bold**.

The company was **founded** / **established** in … / It is **based in** …
The **main activities** of the company are …
It **produces** / **supplies** / **exports** / **manufactures** …
It is **one of the leading** … / **at the forefront of** …
It has an **annual turnover** in excess **of** …
It is **headed by** …
It is **organized into** three divisions / **made up of** five departments

3 Prepare to describe a company you know. Make notes about its background, main activity, structure and organization, etc. Then describe the company in as much detail as you can.

Speak up!

2 Look at the company profile of Drucher Bahn Systems. Use the language above and any other expressions you know for describing an organization to talk about this company.

Company profile Name: Drucher Bahn Systems Established: 1862 Main activity: manufacture of railway vehicles Headquarters: Berlin, Germany Turnover: €575 million p.a. No. of employees: 12,392 Market share: 15%	Managing Director: Hans Kilmer Organization Operations [Design, Maintenance] Production Business Development [Strategy, Project Management], HR Finance Extra information Carriages 20% lighter than competition Rapid growth in recent years

C Listening – Introducing new staff members

1 Look at the sentences below. <u>Underline</u> the expressions you can use to introduce someone.

<u>This is</u> Tony Wilkinson.
Let me introduce you to our General Manager.
Can I introduce you to Sonya?
I'd like you to meet our new marketing director.
I want you to meet the rest of the team.

2 🔵11 Listen to this new member of staff being shown around a company. Tick ✓ the expressions you hear.

3 🔵11 Listen again. Write the correct job next to each person.

Lisa Vickers <u>Accounts Administrator</u>
Carol Parks _____
Tim Starks _____
Helen Green _____

What department do you think all these people work in?

_____

Focus on …
job titles

Do you know what job titles these abbreviations stand for?

1 MD   <u>Managing Director</u>
2 CEO   _____
3 CFO   _____
4 VP   _____
5 CIO   _____
6 COO   _____

D Listening – Roles and responsibilities

1 🎧 12 Listen to four people talk about their jobs. Which department do you think each person works in?

a Finance   b Sales and Marketing   c Human Resources
d Public Relations   e Research and Development   f Customer Services

Michiko ___d___   Carl _____   Youssry _____   Heidi _____

Michiko Hosaka, Japan

Carl Jackson, US

2 🎧 12 Listen again and note any words or expressions that helped you to identify the department each person works in.

Michiko _Promoting the company, raise our profile, image_
Carl _____
Youssry _____
Heidi _____

Youssry Jabber, Kuwait

Heidi Stolz, Germany

E Speaking – Describing your personal qualities

Speaking strategy: Talking about your strengths

1 Study these words and expressions you can use to describe someone's personal qualities.

creative   flexible   determined   efficient
reliable   well-organized   analytical
methodical   confident   sociable

a good listener
good with computers
good at solving problems
can overcome challenges
can work under pressure
able to meet deadlines
good at communicating with people
a good decision maker

Speak up!

2 Look at Michiko, Carl, Youssry and Heidi again. For each person, say what qualities you think they need in order to fulfil their role well.

3 What are your personal qualities? Tick ✓ the qualities in Exercise 1 that you think you possess. Complete the personal profile opposite, then talk about your strengths.

Sound smart
Word stress

1 🎧 13.1 Listen to the word below and answer the questions.
o o O o o
analytical

a How many syllables does the word have?
b Where is the main stress?

2 Now look at these words and write each word in the correct column below.

creative   flexible   determined
efficient   reliable   well-organized
methodical   confident   sociable

oOo	Ooo	oOoo

3 🎧 13.2 Now listen and check. Then listen again and repeat each word. Try to copy the stress.

Personal profile
Personal qualities
_____
_____

Abilities
_____
_____

F Speaking – Talking about your work

Speaking strategy: Describing your job

1 🔘12 Look at the expressions below you can use to describe the work you do. Listen again to Michiko, Carl, Youssry and Heidi describe their jobs. Write M (Michiko), C (Carl), Y (Youssry), and H (Heidi) next to the expressions that each person uses.

I'm in charge of … ☑M
My job involves … ☐ ☐
I'm responsible for … ☐
My main responsibility is to … ☐
I'm interested in … ☐
I'm (mainly) concerned with … ☐

Speak up!

2 **Choose one of the following:**

your current job   a job you once had   a job you'd like to have

Make notes of your role and responsibilities below. Then use your notes to talk about the job.

Company:

Department:

Job title:

Main responsibilities:

Focus on …
prepositions with *work*

Complete each sentence with a preposition.
1 I work __for__ a large international company.
2 I work _____ the sales department.
3 The colleagues I work _____ are very supportive.
4 I work mainly _____ our London office.
5 At the moment I'm working _____ a big project.
6 I have to work _____ very tight deadlines.

Class bonus

Think of a job and make a list of personal qualities needed, and the main responsibilities. Then make a group and describe the job to your classmates. Can they guess the job you are describing?

Extra practice

Choose a company that you are interested in and find out as much as you can about it. Visit their website and listen to any interviews or watch any videos there. Then imagine you are telling a friend about the company. If possible, record what you say and listen to yourself afterwards. Can you identify any areas you could improve, e.g. grammar, pronunciation, etc.?

Can-do checklist

Tick what you can do.

	Can do	Need more practice
I can understand and explain a company's structure and organization.		
I can understand work roles and responsibilities.		
I can talk about my work and what I do in my job.		
I can detail my personal qualities and describe my strengths.		

Unit 9
I'll sort it out

Get ready to listen and speak

- Match each adjective (a–f) with another adjective (1–6) that has a similar meaning.

  a polite   1 tactful
  b flexible   2 well-informed
  c sympathetic   3 dedicated
  d committed   4 caring
  e knowledgeable   5 accommodating
  f diplomatic   6 courteous

- Tick ✓ the three most important qualities you think someone needs to work in Customer Services.

- 'The customer is always right.' Do you agree?

go to Useful language p. 80

A Listening – Handling customer complaints

Did you know …?

According to a survey by the Trading Standards Council, a consumer protection organization in the UK, a customer who receives bad service tells at least nine people, while a customer who gets good service tells only two!

1 🔘14 Listen to two customer services assistants deal with dissatisfied customers on the phone. Complete the chart.

	Conversation 1	Conversation 2
What is the problem?	the customer hasn't received a book he ordered	
What action does the assistant take?		
Is the customer satisfied?		

2 🔘14 Listen again to each conversation and complete the sentences below.

Conversation 1
a I'm very sorry for __the delay__ .
b I'm afraid we've been _____ .
c Please give me a moment and _____ .
d I'll get onto it _____ .

Conversation 2
e I do apologize for _____ .
f I know, but unfortunately we've been having _____ .
g Could you bear with me _____ , please?
h I'll sort it out _____ .

B Speaking – Keeping the customer happy

Speaking strategy: Dealing with complaints

1   Look at the completed sentences in Exercise 2 of Section A. Write the letters of expressions you can use to …

ask someone to be patient ..c.. ......
apologize ....
promise to take action ....
explain the cause of a problem ....

Speak up!

2   🔘15 Imagine you work in a customer services department. Listen and use the ideas below to explain the cause of the problem. Begin with an apology.

Example
You hear: a
           I asked for a brochure a month ago, but I haven't received one yet.
You say: Oh dear. I do apologize. I'm afraid we've run out.

a   run out of brochures
b   very busy this month
c   problems with our website
d   an administrative error
e   the manager is ill today

3   🔘16 Now listen and use the ideas below to promise to take action and say what you will do. Begin with an apology.

Example
You hear: a
           I ordered a set of six wine glasses, but when they arrived three were broken.
You say: I'm very sorry. I'll get onto it immediately. I'll send you another set.

a   send another set
b   book an engineer to fix it
c   arrange to exchange it
d   refund 15%
e   get someone to call you

4   🔘17 Listen and use the ideas below to have a conversation with a customer. Speak after the beeps.

Example
You hear: I paid for a Canon X40 printer online but you've just sent an email saying it's not in stock. a
You say: Yes, I'm very sorry for the delay. I'm afraid it's a very popular model.

a   apologize / explain – (popular model)
b   ask the customer to be patient – (more next Monday)
c   promise action – (send one special delivery)
d   end the call

C Speaking – Getting it right

Speaking strategy: Confirming information

1   Look at these extracts from the conversations in Section A. To confirm information, you can repeat the details and use these expressions.

You want 25 HP356 printer cartridges.
Is that correct?
So, you want six wine glasses.
Is that right?

> ### Learning tip
>
> Remember your voice should go up at the end of a question when you want to check that something is correct. This shows the listener that you are asking for confirmation.

Speak up!

2   Imagine you work in a call centre and are taking orders from customers by phone. Use the ideas below to confirm what each customer wants to order.

Example: a You want to order three large black 'Oxford' suitcases, and you'd like them to be delivered on Friday 15th May, is that correct?

a   Fri 15th May delivery

b

c

d

e   Mon 1st June delivery

Sound smart
Linking – /w/ and /j/

1 **(18)** Listen to these sentences. Notice that a /w/ or /j/ sound is added when a word ending in a vowel sound is followed by a word beginning with a vowel sound.
   a   What would you like to /w/ order?
   b   We can guarantee delivery by the /j/ end of the month.

2 Look at these sentences. Which sounds do you think are linked with /w/ or /j/? There are more than one in some sentences.
   a   I asked you over a month ago for a brochure.
   b   Please give me a moment to check.
   c   I'll get onto it immediately.
   d   We'll post the order special delivery.
   e   I'll post it in the afternoon.
   f   Can I ask who is speaking, please?
   g   I do apologize for all the inconvenience.
   h   You sent me an email to ask about delivery.
   i   I'll be out of the office all next week.

   (19) Listen and check. Then listen again and repeat each sentence. Practise linking the sounds.

Class bonus

Half the class are customer service assistants, the other half are customers.

Customer service assistants: Listen to each customer's complaint and respond by apologizing, explaining the reason for the problem, and promising to take action. You may need to ask some customers to be patient.

Customers: Think of a complaint you have about a product or service. Then speak to various customer service assistants and complain. Try to resolve your complaint.

D Listening – Problems in the office

1 **(20)** Listen and write the number of each speaker (1–6) next to the correct picture (a–f).

2 **(20)** Listen again and complete the expressions.

   a   The air-conditioning's _____on the blink_____ .
   b   This computer _____ .
   c   This printer won't _____ .
   d   I can't get this fax to _____ .
   e   The projector _____ .
   f   This camera won't _____ .

3 What would you do in each situation?

4 🔊**21** Now listen to these replies. Match each reply (1–6) with a problem in Exercise 2 (a–f).

1 __c__   2 _____   3 _____
4 _____   5 _____   6 _____

5 🔊**22** Listen to Pilar and Martin deal with a routine problem at the office. Answer the questions.

a What's the problem?
----

b What do they do?
----

c What was the cause of the problem?

Did you know …?

The top five complaints about offices are:
1 temperature – too cold
2 temperature – too hot
3 poor cleaning service
4 not enough meeting rooms
5 insufficient filing space

E Speaking – Finding solutions

Speaking strategy: Putting forward a solution

1 Look at this extract from Martin and Pilar's conversation. <u>Underline</u> two expressions Pilar uses to put forward a solution.

Pilar: Maybe it means there's some paper stuck inside. It might be worth opening it and having a look.
Martin: How do I do that?
Pilar: You could try pulling that lever there. That's the one.

2 Look at the sentences below and <u>underline</u> two more expressions you can use to propose a solution.

Have you tried switching it off for a few minutes?
What about pressing the reset button?

Speak up!

3 🔊**23** Imagine you are at work and colleagues are telling you about some problems. Listen to each problem and use the ideas below to suggest a solution. Say your answers aloud.

Example
You hear: a
    We've got so many orders we're in danger of falling behind on deliveries.
You say: Well, it might be worth taking on more staff? That might help.

a take on more staff
b ask a technician to look at it
c reduce our prices
d have a special promotion
e give the staff a bonus
f change supplier

E✗tra practice

Listen again to some of the recordings in this unit. For each recording, listen carefully and try to identify a /w/ or /j/ sound. Then look at the Audioscript on pages 92–3 and listen once more to check.

Can-do checklist

Tick what you can do.

	Can do	Need more practice
I can handle customer complaints effectively and in a professional way.		
I can confirm and check important information.		
I can put forward solutions for dealing with general work problems.		

Unit 10
Can I call you back?

go to Useful language p. 81

Get ready to listen and speak

○ How often do you use the telephone to do these things? Tick ✓ your answers.

	Often	Sometimes	Hardly ever
arrange a meeting	☐	☐	☐
deal with complaints	☐	☐	☐
take an order	☐	☐	☐
place an order	☐	☐	☐
find out information	☐	☐	☐
ask someone for help	☐	☐	☐
promote your company's services	☐	☐	☐
apply for a job	☐	☐	☐
answer customers' queries	☐	☐	☐

○ Write *Do* or *Don't* for each phrase below.
Good Telephone Manners

.... sound relaxed
.... eat while you speak
.... be polite
.... use slang words
.... speak quickly
.... speak clearly
.... rush the conversation
.... sound friendly
.... speak naturally
.... continue to work while talking

○ Look at the guide above. Do you think you have good telephone manners?

A Listening – Making a call

1 🔘24 **Listen to two conversations. Answer the questions.**

Conversation 1
a What company is Norman Silvers from?
   Highgate Investments
b Why can't he speak to Mr Fredericks?
   ----
c When should Mr Fredericks be free?
   ----
d What message does he leave?

Conversation 2
e What department does Charlie call?
   ----
f Why does he ask to speak to Sharon?
   ----
g Why isn't Sharon available?
   ----
h What message does he leave?

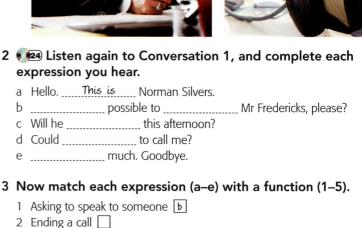

2 🔘24 **Listen again to Conversation 1, and complete each expression you hear.**

a Hello. _____This is_____ Norman Silvers.
b _____ possible to _____ Mr Fredericks, please?
c Will he _____ this afternoon?
d Could _____ to call me?
e _____ much. Goodbye.

3 Now match each expression (a–e) with a function (1–5).

1 Asking to speak to someone b
2 Ending a call ☐
3 Introducing yourself ☐
4 Leaving a message ☐
5 Asking when someone will be available ☐

4 🔊**24** **Listen again to Conversation 2. Write a suitable expression for each function.**

1 Introducing yourself
Hi, it's Charlie.
2 Asking to speak to someone
....
3 Asking when someone will be available
....
4 Leaving a message
....
5 Ending a call
....

5 **Which is more fomal, conversation 1 or 2?** ....

Focus on ...
telephoning

Complete each sentence with a preposition.
a Please don't put me ....on.... hold.
b He's not .... his desk, I'm afraid.
c I'll call you when he gets ....
d She's .... a meeting.
e I'll put you .... right away.
f She's .... another call.
g It's lovely to hear .... you.
h Can I call you .... ?

B Speaking – Making calls successfully

Speaking strategy: Leaving a message

1 **When the person you want to speak to is not available, you can leave a message. Number the steps below (a–f) in order (1–6).**

a repeat your name/company ☐
b end the call ☐
c introduce yourself [1]
d ask when the person will be available ☐
e ask to speak to the person you want ☐
f leave a message ☐

Speak up!

2 🔊**25** **Imagine you work for Suntours International. You phone an important client at Richmond Travel Ltd. Use the ideas below to have a formal conversation with the receptionist and leave a message.**

Example
You hear: Hello, Richmond Travel Ltd. a
You say: Hello. This is [your name] from Suntours International. Would it be possible to speak with Catherine Simmons, please?

a You are [your name] from Suntours International. You want to speak to Catherine Simmons. ·
b available this afternoon?
c can she call you asap?
d Repeat your name and company. Give your mobile number: 07967 324094.
e end the call

3 🔊**26** **Imagine you phone the Personnel department in your company, but the person you want to speak to is not available. Use the ideas below to have an informal conversation with another colleague and leave a message.**

Example
You hear: Hello, Personnel. a
You say: Hi, it's [your name]. Is Trisha there?

a Give your name. You want to speak to Trisha.
b when will be back?
c say I called?
d give your extension – 344
e end the call

Learning tip

Before you make an important call, it is a good idea to make a list of the points you want to raise. Make sure you have all the information you need. Have a pen and some paper ready in case you need to make notes.

Did you know …?

Using the phone effectively is a valuable skill. Some small companies even employ professional agencies to deal with all their telephone calls. Surveys show that people respond more positively to someone with good telephone manners.

C Listening – Receiving a call

1 🔊**27** Listen to two conversations. Which conversation (1 or 2) is more formal? _____

2 🔊**27** Listen again and complete each expression below.

1 Hello, Tim ___speaking___ .
2 Can I take _____ ?
3 Hang on. I'll _____ his office for you.
4 No, sorry. The _____ .
5 Hello. _____ Jane Garston.
6 _____ to leave a message?
7 I'll just put _____ .
8 I'm afraid he's _____ right now.

3 Match each expression (1–8) in Exercise 2 with a function (a–d).

a Answering the phone 1, _____
b Saying someone isn't available _____
c Connecting someone _____
d Offering to take a message _____

D Speaking – Practise receiving calls

Speaking strategy: Handling incoming calls effectively

1 When you answer a call and the person the caller asks for is not available, you can ask if they want to leave a message. Look at the steps below and number each step (a–f) in order (1–6).

a offer to connect the caller ☐
b end the call ☐
c answer the phone ☐1☐
d offer to take a message ☐
e ask the caller (to confirm) their name ☐
f say the person isn't available ☐

Speak up!

2 🔊**28** Imagine someone calls and asks to talk to your colleague at work. Listen and reply, using the ideas below.

Example
You hear: Oh, hello. I'd like to speak to Françoise Chirac, please. a
You say: I'll just put you through.

a put you through   c a message?   e end the call
b on another line   d caller's name?

3 🔊**29** Imagine you take a call from a colleague in another department. The person they want to speak to is not available. Listen and reply, using the ideas below. Have an informal conversation and take a message.

Example
You hear: Hi, Nigel. It's Samantha. Is George there? a
You say: Hang on. I'll try his office for you.

a try his office   c a message?   e end the call
b engaged   d confirm caller's name?

Sound smart
Connected speech

1 🔊**30** When words are spoken together in English they are often pronounced differently than when said on their own. Look at these examples. Listen and notice how the sounds change:

a <u>Do you</u> /djə/ know when she'll be back?
b <u>Would you</u> /wudjə/ like to leave a message?
c <u>Could you</u> /kudjə/ tell her I called?
d <u>Do you</u> /djə/ <u>want to</u> /wontə/ call back later?
e When's the meeting <u>going to</u> /gonə/ finish?

2 🔊**30** Listen again and repeat each sentence. Try to copy the same sounds and rhythm.

3 🔊**31** Listen to five more sentences. How many words do you hear in each sentence? Write the number of words you hear. Contractions such as *you're* count as two words.
a ☐10☐ b ☐ c ☐
d ☐ e ☐
Listen again and write each sentence in full.

4 🔊**31** Now practise. Listen and repeat each sentence.

E Listening – Overcoming difficulties

1 Look at the picture below. Why do you think the woman is having difficulty understanding what the man is saying?

Sorry. I didn't quite catch that.

2 🎧 32 Listen to five people speaking on the phone. Why is it difficult to understand each speaker? Match each speaker (a–e) with a reason (1–5).

1 The speaker has an unfamiliar name. ☐
2 There is too much background noise. ☐
3 The speaker is talking too softly. [a]
4 The speaker gives too much information all at once. ☐
5 The line quality is poor. ☐

3 🎧 33 Now listen and complete each sentence you hear.

a Would you mind _spelling that_ for me?
b Sorry. Can you _____ again?
c Could you _____ , please?
d I think we have _____ . I'll call you back.
e Could you speak _____ , please?

4 🎧 34 Imagine you take the following five calls. Listen and use one of the expressions above to help overcome each difficulty you come up against.

Example: a Can you speak up, please?

Class bonus

In pairs, role play various telephone conversations. Sit back to back, or use your mobile phones to talk to each other. Choose formal and informal situations, e.g. answering queries from an important client, or asking a colleague for information. Decide on a situation and prepare your call first, then practise.

E✗tra practice

Some companies have free numbers that you can call to ask about products and services. Think of some questions to ask, then call and find out what you can. Use the language and strategies in this unit to help you. Why not ring a company after hours and listen to their recorded message? You could practise taking notes of the important information and ring back if you need to listen again.

Can-do checklist

Tick what you can do.

	Can do	Need more practice
I can make and take calls effectively.		
I can take and leave messages.		
I can overcome common difficulties when speaking by phone.		

Unit 11
Shall we move on?

Get ready to **listen and speak**

- Look at these factors that help to contribute towards an effective meeting. Tick ✓ the three that you think are the most important.
  - There is a written agenda. ☐
  - The meeting is controlled well. ☐
  - The meeting starts on time. ☐
  - People respect each other's opinions. ☐
  - There is sufficient time to get through everything. ☐
  - Everyone gets to express their opinion. ☐
  - Everyone is there who needs to be. ☐
  - The aims of the meeting are clear. ☐
  - The meeting achieves its objectives. ☐

- Make a note of three things you need to do to chair a meeting effectively.

  ----

go to Useful language p. 81

A Listening – Starting a meeting

1 🔊 **35** **David is Managing Director of Avocet Industries, a large international chemical company. He is chairing an important strategy meeting. Listen to him start the meeting and complete the expressions he uses below.**

   a Perhaps we can _____*get started*_____ .
   b First, _____ you all for coming.
   c I'd _____ welcome …
   d The _____ this meeting is to …
   e You _____ the agenda that …

2 **Write the letter of each expression (a–e) next to the correct function (1–5).**

   1 referring people to the agenda `e`
   2 getting everyone's attention ☐
   3 welcoming people ☐
   4 thanking people ☐
   5 explaining the aims of the meeting ☐

3 **What other expressions can you think of that you could use for the above functions? Make a list.**

   ----

4 🔊 **35** **Now write T (true) or F (false) for each statement. Then listen again and check.**

   a The meeting will last two days. __T__
   b Javier is the only representative from Spain. ____
   c Inessa interrupted her holiday to attend the meeting. ____
   d The meeting has been called because of recent poor performance. ____
   e There are only two issues to discuss at the meeting. ____

B Listening – Identifying opinions

1 [CD 36] Listen to this extract from later in the meeting. The item being discussed is a proposal to close the company's operations in France and Germany. What does each person think of the suggestion? Tick ✓ your answers.

	Agrees	Disagrees	Partly agrees
David			
Inessa	✓		
Javier			
Ian			

2 Unscramble the expressions each person uses to give their opinion.

a to / I / extent / some / agree
  I agree to some extent.

b not / it / completely / I'm / to / opposed
  _____

c way / see / I / pros / can / cons / each / and
  _____

d favour / it / I'm / of / in
  _____

e all / I'm / the / keen / very / idea / not / on / at
  _____

3 [CD 36] Look at the functions below, then listen again and write a suitable expression you hear for each function.

1 Interrupting
  Sorry, can I come in here? ....

2 Expressing reservations
  ....

3 Making a suggestion
  ....

4 Accepting a suggestion
  ....

5 Rejecting a suggestion
  ....

4 Now look at these expressions. Match each one (a–e) with a function (1–5) above.

a I know what you mean, but … [2]
b I'd like to say something if I may. [ ]
c I'll go along with that. [ ]
d We might want to … [ ]
e I think that would be a mistake. [ ]

Learning tip

When you are in a meeting, you need to be sure you understand the opinions of those around you. Listen out for key expressions like those in B above that can help you understand what people are thinking. If you can follow the discussion more closely, you'll be able to participate more.

Did you know …?

A survey by the *Wall Street Journal* found that most managers spend an average of 15 hours a week in meetings, but only 56% said the meetings were productive!

Focus on …
the language of meetings

Match each word or phrase (1–8) with a definition (a–h).

1 agenda   a to put forward a plan for consideration
2 to second   b to express your choice or opinion (by raising your hand, etc.)
3 minutes   c a list of matters to be discussed
4 vote   d a formal suggestion
5 to propose   e a list of things that need to be done after the meeting
6 motion   f the person who leads the meeting
7 action points   g to formally give your support to a suggestion
8 chair   h a written record of what was said or decided

C Speaking – Acting as chair

Speaking strategy: Controlling a meeting

1 Look at this list of things a chair has to do. Match each responsibility
(1–5) with two expressions (a–j).

a I don't think [name] has finished yet.
b I'm not sure that's relevant here.
c We need to look at this in more detail.

1 Deal with interruptions _a_ _____
2 Keep to the point _____ _____
3 Speed things up _____ _____
4 Slow things down _____ _____
5 Summarize the main decisions _____ _____

d Let's go over what we've agreed.
e Could you let [name] finish, please?
f Perhaps we should discuss this a bit more.
g I think we're drifting off the point a bit.
h Shall we move on?
i OK, to sum up then …
j Does anyone have anything else to add?

2 🔵36 Listen again to the extract from the
meeting between David, Inessa, Javier
and Ian. Tick ✓ the expressions in Exercise 1
that you hear David use.

Speak up!

3 Imagine you are the chair of a meeting. Look
at the situations below. Use the expressions
above to control the meeting.

Example: a
You say: I don't think Carol has finished yet.

a Carol is speaking but Jeremy tries to interrupt.
b An important decision needs to be made and people
seem unclear about the options.
c The aim of the meeting is to decide overtime pay but
holiday entitlement is dominating the discussion.
d You feel the discussion has focused on one point for
too much time.
e You want to draw the meeting to a close.

Sound smart
Using stress to emphasize a contrast

1 🔵37 Listen to this extract from the meeting.
Underline the words that Ian stresses.
a We need to expand our European operations, not
close them down!

2 🔵37 Now listen again and ⊙circle the correct answer
to complete the rules below.

When you want to emphasize a contrast you should …
… say the relevant words *louder* / *softer* than the
other words.

3 Underline the words you want to contrast in these
sentences, then practise saying the sentences
stressing these words.
a Sales should be <u>increasing</u>, not <u>falling</u>.
b We need our staff to work longer hours, not
shorter.
c We should be hiring staff, not firing them.
d We need more skilled labour, not unskilled labour.
e We need to be more competitive, not more
expensive.

🔵38 Now listen and repeat each sentence. Try to
copy the stress and intonation as closely as you can.

D Speaking – Avoiding conflict

Speaking strategy: Being diplomatic

1 Study these ways you can express your opinion in a softer way to avoid offending other people. Then match each example (a–d) with a strategy (1–4) you can use.

a Your opinion: The sales campaign was disappointing.
  You say: *Would it be fair to say the sales campaign wasn't as good as we'd hoped?*

b Your opinion: It was a terrible decision.
  You say: *I'm not sure it was a very good decision.*

c Your opinion: The sales figures were extremely disappointing.
  You say: *The sales figures seemed rather disappointing.*

d Your opinion: The project was a waste of money.
  You say: *On the whole, the project didn't deliver good value for money.*

1 Avoid negative adjectives by using a negative verb with a positive adjective. __b__
2 Reduce the strength of what you say, e.g. *extremely → rather.* ......
3 Turn a statement into a question. ......
4 Use general and cautious language, e.g. *on the whole, in general, tend to, might*, etc. ......

2 **You can combine two or more strategies to help avoid causing offence. Look at the examples below. How many strategies can you find?**

Your opinion: These meetings are a waste of time.
You say: *These meetings don't tend to be particularly useful.*

Your opinion: Our performance was poor.
You say: *Would you agree that on the whole, our performance wasn't very good?*

Speak up!

3 Imagine you are in a meeting and want to express the following opinions. Use the strategies above to make your opinions sound less critical.

Example: a
You say: Would it be fair to say that on the whole the product launch didn't go very well?

a The product launch went badly.
b Sales have been terrible.
c Customers think the quality is poor.
d The senior management are to blame.
e The company's reputation has suffered a lot.

Class bonus

Make a group. You are going to hold a meeting. Decide together on the topic of the meeting. Then choose who will be the chair, and decide what roles everyone else will have. Now role play the meeting. Use the language and strategies in this unit to help you.

E X tra practice

Watch a current affairs programme in English on satellite or cable TV, or listen to a debate on a radio programme in English. Notice the language the people use during their discussion.

Can-do checklist

Tick what you can do.

	Can do	Need more practice
I can identify other people's opinions.		
I can contribute to a meeting as a participant.		
I can lead a meeting effectively as chair.		
I can express my own opinions diplomatically.		

Unit 12
I'd like to begin by ...

Get ready to listen and speak

- Look at these different ways of taking notes. Which do you think is best?
- Do you use a system like the ones below when you take notes?

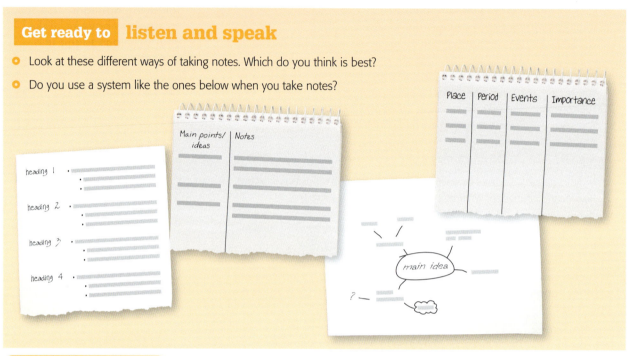

go to Useful language p. 81

A Listening – Do's and don'ts

1 🔊 **439** Listen to this lecturer give some advice to her students on taking notes in class. Make a note of the advice she gives in the chart below.

Do's	Don'ts
decide what is important	note everything

Did you know …?

The best time to review your notes is within 24 hours of a lecture. Studies show that after this time it is more difficult to remember important details.

2 🔊 **439** Look at the questions below. Answer as many as you can from memory, then listen again and check.

a What does she say a lecture is *not*?

----

b What should you do to be an active listener …? before the lecture

----

during the lecture

----

c In what two ways do lecturers often repeat themselves?

----

d What four things should you do when you review your notes?

----

e What two advantages does she mention of reviewing notes?

Focus on ...
arrows, symbols and abbreviations

ab C def

You can use arrows, symbols and abbreviations to help reduce the amount you need to write. This will save time and allow you to keep up with the lecturer.

1 Look at the arrows, symbols and abbreviations below. Match each one with a meaning (1–16).

e.g. imp. temp. msg ✓ = ↑ yr. vs. etc. ✗ ↓ poss + C info

1 in addition to ......
2 for example ......
3 important ......
4 and so on ......
5 message ......
6 go up/rise ......
7 a negative point ......
8 Century ......
9 go down/fall ......
10 a positive/good point ......
11 possible ......
12 temperature ......
13 versus/against ......
14 the same as ......
15 information ......
16 year ......

2 You can also make up your own symbols and abbreviations to help you take notes more quickly. For example, @ (*about/around*), tk (*take*), lrn (*learn*). Make a list of non-standard abbreviations you like to use. Try to think of some more to add to the list.

3 Look at your notes in the Do's/Don'ts chart. Can you make them more concise?

Learning tip

Active listening is a useful skill when taking notes. Decide what is important and what is not and listen for any guidance the lecturer gives you. For example, notice when a lecturer repeats something, and make sure you note the point down.

B Listening – Note taking

1 🔘40 **Listen to an extract from a lecture on the Chinese economy. After each section, pause the recording and choose the most suitable heading.**

1 a China 40 years ago
  ⓑ Background to economic success
2 a Influence of the US
  b Growth statistics
3 a A growing population
  b A population on the move
4 a Economic deficiencies
  b Labour costs
5 a More growth ahead
  b Future challenges

2 🔘40 **Write each heading in place in the notepad. Then listen again and make notes under each heading. Be concise, numbering points, and using arrows, symbols or abbreviations where you can.**

3 **Review your notes. How concise are they? Do they contain all the key information? Can you improve them?**

China's economy

1

2

3

4

5

C Speaking – Passing information on

Speaking strategy: Talking about a lecture

1 Here are some expressions you can use to talk about a lecture and pass on information:

The talk was about … / The speaker began by …ing / Then she argued that … / After that she reviewed/mentioned … / Then she went on to say that… / Finally she … / I think the most important/interesting/relevant point was …

Speak up!

2 Give an oral summary of the extract from the lecture on China you heard. Use your notes to help you.

> ### Learning tip
>
> A good summary should not try to repeat everything, but simply cover the most important points, together with some details of particular interest to the person giving the summary. It should be well-organized, easy to understand and accurate.

D Listening – Summarizing

1 🔊 **41** Listen to two summaries of the talk you heard. Which one (a or b) do you think is better? _____

2 🔊 **41** Listen again and make a note of the strengths and weaknesses of each summary.

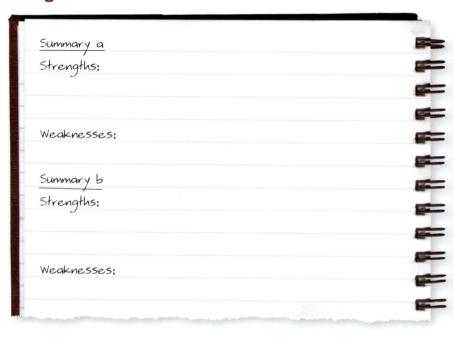

Summary a
Strengths:

Weaknesses:

Summary b
Strengths:

Weaknesses:

E Listening – Time for questions

1 🔊 **42** Listen to four people each ask a question at the end of a lecture. Note the key point that each person (a–d) is asking about.

a mass migration
b _____
c _____
d _____

2 🔊 **43** Now listen to the replies (1–4). Match each reply (1–4) with a question (a–d).

1 c   2 _____   3 _____   4 _____

3 🔊 **43** Listen again to the replies and complete the expressions that the lecturer uses to clarify what she means.

a Basically, what I want _____ to say _____ is …
b I suppose what I'm _____ is …
c The point I'm _____ is …
d In other words, what I'm _____ is …

F Speaking – Asking questions

Speaking strategy: Asking for clarification

1 Look at the questions below and <u>underline</u> each expression you can use to ask for clarification.

a <u>Could you explain what you mean by</u> the biggest mass migration in history?
b Can you go into a bit more detail on the cost of labour in China?
c What exactly are you getting at when you refer to the middle class as the 'backbone of China's success'?
d Would you expand a little on the impact of China's economic growth?

Speak up!

2 Imagine you want to ask a lecturer for clarification. Use the ideas below, and say your answers aloud.

Example: a, current economic position – more detail
You say: Can you go into a bit more detail on the current economic position?

a current economic position – more detail
b economic superpower – explain?
c 'draining effect' of migration from countryside to cities – getting at?
d environmental cost of economic success – expand
e skill shortage – explain?
f causes of rising inflation – more detail

Learning tip

It may be possible to take a tape recorder into the lecture and record everything the lecturer says. This is useful to refer to afterwards when you review your notes. Always ask the lecturer's permission first.

E X tra practice

Go to the website below and listen to a lecture that interests you. Note the main ideas and then review your notes afterwards by reading the text of the lecture.
http://www.thersa.org/audio/

Class bonus

Choose two volunteers from the class to each give a short talk on any topic they like. The talk should last no more than two minutes. Each speaker should tell the class the topic of their talk.
Decide which talk you want to listen to. Then divide into two groups and listen to the talk you chose, taking notes of the main points. When the talk finishes, compare your notes with the other students in your group. Finally, find a classmate who listened to the other talk and each give a summary.

Can-do checklist

Tick what you can do.

	Can do	Need more practice
I can take effective notes in a talk or lecture.		
I can give an accurate and concise summary of the main points.		
I can ask detailed questions for further information.		

Unit 13
Let's take a closer look

Get ready to listen and speak

● Look at the graphics below. Which ways of presenting visual information can you see? Choose from the list.

a line graph   a flow chart   a pie chart   a bar chart   a diagram   a table   a plan

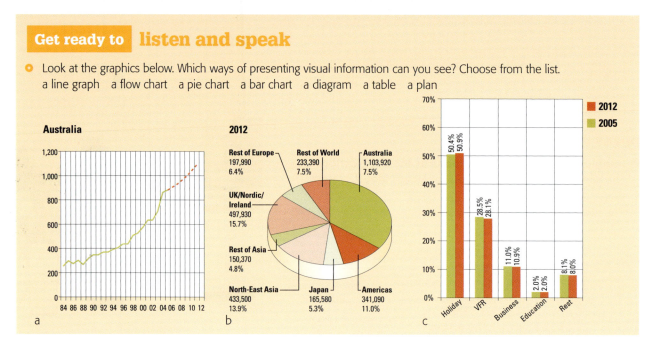

a   b   c

go to Useful language p. 82

A Listening – Charts and statistics

1 🔘44 Kirsty McLellan works for the Ministry of Tourism in New Zealand. She is giving a talk to her colleagues on some recent research.

Listen and number each presentation slide (a–c) above in the order (1–3) Kirsty mentions them.

a ....   b ....   c ....

2 🔘44 Listen again. Tick ✓ the main topic of each slide.

a The importance of tourism to New Zealand ☐
   International visitor arrivals ☐
   Market strengths and weaknesses ☐

b The history of the Australian market ☐
   Reasons for growth of the Australian market ☐
   The importance of the Australian market ☐

c New Zealand's secret of success ☐
   Reasons for travel to New Zealand ☐
   The best place for a holiday ☐

3 🔘44 Answer these questions from memory, then listen again and check.

a Which four countries do most tourists come from?
   ----

b What two factors have helped the Australian market?
   ----

c What is the predicted rate of growth?
   ----

d What activities are most tourists on holiday interested in?
   ----

e What does VFR mean in the bar chart?

Focus on ...
describing statistics

1 Match each word or expression (a–h) with a graph (1–8).

a increase sharply _8_ b go up slightly _____ c fluctuate _____ d fall steadily _____
e recover well _____ f drop dramatically _____ g level out _____ h remain steady _____

2 Match a verb in A with a verb in B which has a similar meaning.

A	B
1 climb	a even out
2 decrease	b reach
3 pick up	c get worse
4 stabilize	d rise
5 deteriorate	e decline
6 get up to	f improve

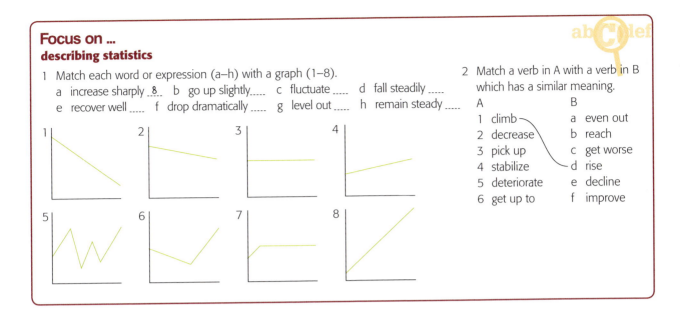

B Speaking – Presenting detailed information

Speaking strategy: Describing charts and graphs

1 **Complete these expressions you can use to introduce information on a chart by adding the correct words.**

shows   As you   notice
this chart   draw   can see

a You'll ___notice___ that …
b You can see from _____ that …
c This graph _____ …
d What we _____ here is …
e _____ can see from …
f I'd like to _____ your attention to …

Speak up!

2 **Repeat Kirsty's talk on tourism in New Zealand in your own words. Refer to the presentation slides on page 60, and use the language above to help you.**

Did you know …?

Experts say around 80% of what we learn is learned visually. Using visual aids such as graphs and charts is an extremely effective way of getting your point across.

3 **Look at the slides below from the next part of Kirsty's talk. Imagine you are giving the talk. What can you say about each slide?**

Visitor arrivals (000s)

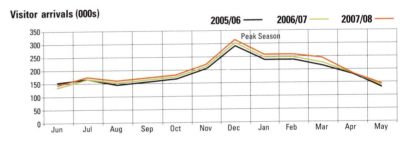

Total expenditure ($NZm)

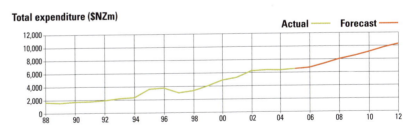

Growth in visitor arrivals (%)
Annual Change

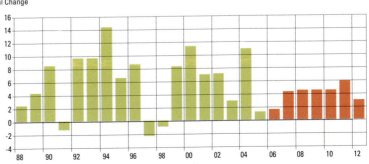

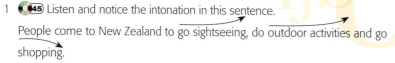

Sound smart
Mentioning several points

1 (45) Listen and notice the intonation in this sentence.

People come to New Zealand to go sightseeing, do outdoor activities and go shopping.

2 Now (circle) the correct words to complete the rule.

If you want to list several points one after the other, your voice should go *up* / *down* on the first two examples, and then go *up* / *down* on the final example.

3 (45) Listen again and practise.

4 Look at these statements and predict where your voice should go up and down.
   a Great Britain is made up of three countries: England, Scotland and Wales.
   b Wales is popular for walking, its great beaches and its many castles.
   c In Scotland tourists visit Edinburgh, Loch Ness and enjoy the great scenery.
   d Popular tourist destinations in England are the Lake District, Cornwall and of course London.
   e London's top attractions include the London Eye, the Tower of London and Buckingham Palace.
   f Three popular museums are the National Gallery, the British Museum and the Tate Modern.

5 (46) Listen and check. Then listen and repeat each sentence. Try to use the same rise-rise-fall intonation.

Learning tip

When you give a talk using detailed statistics and charts, try to explain the information in each chart in a clear and methodical way. Introduce each chart, and use plenty of signposts to help the audience follow what you are saying.

C Speaking – Using signposts (1)

Speaking strategy: Linking ideas

1 **Write each word or expression next to the correct function.**

although	also	furthermore	however
in addition	whereas	despite	moreover

Linking supporting ideas: _in addition,_ ....
Contrasting different ideas: ....

Speak up!

2 **Imagine you are giving a presentation. Introduce the information on each chart and link the ideas.**

Example: a
You say: As you can see from this chart, sales increased in April and furthermore profits also went up.

Focus on ...
expressing contrast

Choose the correct answer to complete each sentence.
   a The company's profits were good *although* / (despite) a slow start.
   b We decided to expand our European operations *even though* / *in spite of* advice to the contrary.
   c The results were poor. *However,* / *Even though* there were no redundancies.
   d *Although* / *In spite of* performance was rather disappointing, the board remained optimistic.
   e The management had a pay rise, *whereas* / *in spite of* the workers' salaries were cut.
   f *However* / *Even though* we have reduced our prices, sales have not gone up.

a April results

b May results

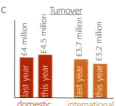

c Turnover

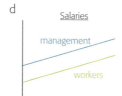

d Salaries

e Customer service

D Listening – Using signposts (2)

1 You are going to listen to a presentation on ice cream sales. Before you listen, look at the functions below and make a list of expressions you might hear.

a Explaining causes and consequences ....

....

b Giving an example ....

c Repeating the same idea ....

....

d Summarizing the main points ....

....

2 🔊47 Now listen to four extracts from the presentation and tick ✓ any expressions in your list you hear.

3 🔊47 Listen again and write any expressions you have not already noted. Write each expression below the correct function.

E Speaking – Making your point

Speaking strategy: Giving verbal cues

1 Match each expression (a–f) with a function (1–3).

1 Finishing one point __b__ ......
2 Starting another point ....
3 Emphasizing an important point ....

a The crucial point here is …
b We've looked at …
c Let me turn to …
d The thing to remember is …
e Let's move on to …
f I've told you about …

Class bonus

1 Prepare a short talk on a topic you know a lot about using graphics.
2 Give your presentation to the class. Use the language and strategies in this unit to help you.

EXtra practice

Listen to a talk in English on the radio or on TV. Notice the language the speaker uses and make a list of any signposts you hear.

Speak up!

2 Imagine you are giving a presentation. Use the ideas below to finish one point, start another and emphasize important points.

Example: a
You say: OK, so we've looked at turnover. Now let me turn to sales. The thing to remember is the sales team is much smaller now.

a turnover / sales – sales team much smaller
b productivity / profit – corporation tax up 2%
c staff levels / salaries – no pay rises for two years
d domestic maketing / international marketing – big cultural differences
e workforce / management – fewer women than men

Can-do checklist

Tick what you can do.

	Can do	Need more practice
I can understand detailed information and statistics.		
I can describe information in charts and graphs clearly and concisely.		
I can use signpost words to link ideas effectively.		

Unit 14
Can you expand on that?

go to Useful language p. 82

Get ready to **listen and speak**

○ Write T (true) or F (false) for each statement.
   a A seminar is an opportunity for a group of students to explore various topics with a teacher. ......
   b Students often take turns to give short talks. ......
   c There is a lot of discussion. Students should express their opinions openly. ......
   d The teacher can take a 'back seat', leaving students in control. ......

○ Have you ever been to a seminar? If so, what do you think of seminars? Tick ✓ your answers.
   a I like seminars. I enjoy debating issues with other students. ☐
   b I think seminars are a waste of time. I want to learn from a teacher, not other students. ☐
   c I find it hard to express my opinion in a group. ☐
   d Seminars are frustrating because one or two people always do all the talking. ☐
   e Seminars are fun but I don't know if they help me learn anything. ☐
   f I don't like to argue with people. I think it's rude. ☐

A Listening – Following a discussion

1 🔵48 **Listen to this extract from a seminar. What do you think is the main topic that the students are discussing?**
   a The decline of minority languages
   b The benefits of language education
   c The preservation of languages
   d The role of government in language development
   e The problem of poverty throughout the world

2 **Now answer these questions.**
   a Is the discussion well-balanced or one-sided?
   ----
   b Is the tone of the discussion friendly, heated, or a bit of both?
   ----
   c Does everyone get an equal chance to express their opinion?

Learning tip

When you are trying to follow a discussion between several people, try not to focus on individuals or specific details too much. Try to 'step back' mentally, and notice how the discussion develops as a whole. Listen to the general flow of the discussion rather than specific details.

3 🔘48 **How does the discussion develop? Look at these areas (a–e) then listen again and number each in order (1–5).**

a conflict between saving people and saving languages ☐
b examples of dying languages ☐1
c reasons to protect languages ☐
d reasons *not* to protect languages ☐
e languages that are reviving ☐

4 🔘48 **Answer these questions. Then listen again and check.**

a According to the UNESCO report
   – how many languages are there in the world today? _____
   – how many are in danger of dying out by 2100? _____
b Where do speakers of the Ainu and Maori languages live? _____
c How many Welsh speakers were there in 1991? How many are there today? _____
d What are the arguments in favour of 'language revitalization'?
   _____
e What are the arguments against language revitalization?
   _____

B Speaking – Expressing your ideas

Speaking strategy: Disagreeing politely

1 Look at these extracts from the seminar discussion. Which expressions (1–4) can you use to …

a disagree about facts?
b disagree about opinions?

1 I don't quite see it like that. __b__
2 I think you might be mistaken on that point. _____
3 I'm not sure I agree. _____
4 I don't think you've got that right. _____

Sound smart
Sounding polite

As well as being careful with the language you use, you can also try to make sure the *way* you say something sounds polite.

1 🔘51 Listen to this sentence spoken twice. Which way (A or B) sounds more polite? Why?

   I think you might be mistaken on that point.

2 🔘52 Listen to each of these sentences repeated twice. Circle which is more polite, A or B.

   I'm not sure you've got that right.   A   B
   That's not quite how I see it.   A   B
   I'm not sure I agree.   A   B
   Sorry, can I finish what I was saying?   A   B

   🔘52 Now listen and practise saying each sentence politely.

Speak up!

2 🔘49 **Imagine you are in a seminar. Listen and use the ideas below to disagree politely about the facts you hear.**

Example
You hear: a
           English is the most widely-spoken language in the world.
You say: I don't think you've got that right. I think it's Chinese.

a Chinese
b 3,500 years ago
c one third
d top to bottom, and right to left
e Basque
f Portuguese

3 🔘50 **Now listen and use the ideas below to disagree politely about the opinions you hear.**

Example
You hear: a
           English is a really difficult language to learn.
You say: I'm not sure I agree. I think it's quite easy.

a quite easy
b depends on the individual
c too expensive
d less interesting
e closely connected
f more people

C Speaking – Making sure you understand

Speaking strategy: Asking for more detail

1 <u>Underline</u> the expressions you can use to ask someone to explain a point in more detail.

<u>Do you think you could say a bit more about</u> that, please?
I'd like to hear more about the impact of English on world languages, if possible.
Do you have any specific details about the decline in minority languages?
Can you give an example of a language that is enjoying a revival?

Speak up!

2 Look at the situations below and ask politely for more detail.

Example: a
You say: Do you think you could say a bit more about the impact of English on other languages?

a impact of English on other languages?
b endangered languages?
c language revitalization?
d rate of decline of minority languages?
e threats to African languages?
f future of language development?

D Listening – Asking effective questions

1 You can repeat a question in a different way to make sure others understand what you are asking, or to focus your question more precisely. Use these words to complete the expressions you can use below.

words asking Basically another suppose

1 In other _____words_____, I'd like to know …
2 _____, what I want to know is …
3 I guess what I'm (really) _____ is …
4 To put it _____ way …
5 I _____ what I'm driving at is …

2 🔘53 Now listen to questions 1–5 and check.

3 🔘53 Look at the questions (a–e) below. Then listen and match each question you hear (1–5) with an original question (a–e).

a Will English always be the dominant world language? ☐
b What are the main reasons for the success of the English language? ☐1☐
c Is it unavoidable that certain languages die out? ☐
d Do you think all languages have equal significance? ☐
e Why do you think the issue of language revitalization is not more in the public eye? ☐

E Listening – Participating effectively

1 🔘 **54) Listen and complete each expression. Then listen and repeat.**

a Sorry, what ___do you mean___ exactly?
b I agree with some _____ said.
c No, sorry. I don't really _____ that.
d I _____ that it's important.
e That's _____ too.
f Can we get _____ here, please?
g My mistake. I _____ . Sorry.
h That's not really _____ .
i OK. So what _____ is …
j What do _____ , Peter?
k Sorry, can I just _____ was saying?
l Can I _____ here?

2 Now match each expression (a–l) with a function (1–12).

1 Ask someone for their opinion ☐ j
2 Ask someone to explain what they mean ☐
3 Ask to interrupt ☐
4 Stop someone from interrupting you ☐
5 Apologize for misunderstanding someone ☐
6 Try to get the discussion back on target ☐
7 Agree with someone ☐
8 Disagree with someone ☐
9 Partly agree with someone ☐
10 Check you've understood ☐
11 Say someone has misunderstood you ☐
12 Give your opinion strongly ☐

3 Add any other expressions you can think of for these functions.

_____
_____
_____
_____

Class bonus

Make a group and have your own seminar. Choose a topic, consider your opinion and then begin a discussion. Participate as fully as you can, asking questions, giving opinions and using the language and strategies covered in this unit. Remember to be polite when disagreeing with someone!

E✗tra practice

Turn to page 95 and find recording script 48. Listen again and read at the same time. Underline any expressions people use for the functions above. Listen again and notice how speakers A and D emphasize the important words and expressions.

Can-do checklist

Tick what you can do.

	Can do	Need more practice
I can follow the development of a lively discussion.		
I can express my opinion and disagree politely.		
I can ask for more detail if necessary.	✓	✓
I can use a range of techniques to participate effectively.		

Unit 15
It'll help me get a good job

Get ready to | listen and speak

- Would you like to study abroad?
- What country would you go to?
- What would you study?

go to Useful language p. 82

A Listening – Making plans

🔘55 Listen to Stefania from Italy and Habib from Saudi Arabia each talk about their study plans for the future. Make notes, and find three goals they share.

Stefania

Habib

B Speaking – Talking about your study plans

Speaking strategy: Describing plans in detail

1 Look at these expressions you can use to describe what you are going to do and hope to achieve in the future.

I plan/aim/intend to …
My/The (main) focus/goal/purpose is to …
I hope/expect it'll help me to …
What I hope to achieve/accomplish/get from this is …

2 🔘55 Listen again to Stefania and Habib. Tick ✓ the expressions they use.

Speak up!

3 Look at the advertisement for San Francisco Language Center. Imagine you are going to study on this programme. Talk about what you are going to do and what you hope to achieve.

SAN FRANCISCO LANGUAGE CENTER

American Language and Culture Program

Dates: July/August

Accommodation: live with a host family

– improve your English
  26 hrs per week, practise communication skills, become more confident

– discover the real US
  learn about US culture, history, people, lifestyles

– make new friends with people from all around the world!

Class bonus

Make a group and talk about your study plans. What do you plan to do? What do you hope to achieve?

C Speaking – Seeking advice

**Speaking strategy:
Asking for opinions and
recommendations**

1 Look at the expressions
below you can use to
ask for opinions and
recommendations.

Would you recommend …ing?
Do you think it's worth …ing?
Is it a good idea to …?
Do you think I should …?
What do you think of …?

Speak up!

2 🔘56 Imagine you are thinking of going on a study trip to
Britain. Listen and use the ideas below to have a conversation
with your English teacher. Ask for your teacher's opinions and
recommendations.

Example
You hear: Yes, do you want to ask me something? a
You say: Yes. Do you think it's worth going to the UK next summer to study
English?

a UK next summer – study English?
b 1 month or 2 months?
c London or Cambridge?
d host family or hotel?
e 15 or 28 hrs per week?
f General English or an exam (IELTS/TOEFL)?
g US or Australia instead?

D Listening – Understanding course requirements

1 🔘57 Imagine you are starting a
business course at college in the
United States. Listen to the college
professor and write T (true) or F
(false) for each statement.

a There are five written assignments. F
b Some assignments can be handed in
late. ......
c There are two exams. ......
d Students have to do a 20-minute oral
report. ......
e There are 25 classes. ......
f It is possible for all students to get
an A. ......

2 🔘57 Listen again and complete
the form.

Module 3.2 *The development of the EU*

Grading system
__30__ % Mid-term exam
_____ % Final exam
_____ % Written assignments
_____ % Oral report
_____ % Preparedness/participation

Grades
A _____
B _____
C _____
D _____
F _____

3 🔘57 Now answer these questions. Then listen once more and check.

a How many per cent of the final grade does each written report represent?
....
b How are the exams organized? _____
c What is the format of the oral report? _____
d What is the attendance requirement? _____

E Listening – A tour of the library

1 🔘58 Robert Armstrong is a librarian at a university library. Listen as he shows a group of new students around the library. Find three mistakes in the information below.

Library opening times:

(during term)	Mon – Fri	9 am – 7 pm
	Sat	9 am – 5.30 pm
	Sun	Closed
(at other times)	Mon – Fri	10 am – 1 pm
	Sat	10 am – 1 pm
	Sun	Closed

No admittance 50 mins before closing

2 🔘59 Now listen and note what you can find in each of these sections of the library.

a Reading Room *articles and journals*
b North Wing ....
c Green Room ....
d South Wing ....

3 🔘59 Answer these questions. Then listen again and check.

a Which locations contain material for reference only?
....

b What must you have to use the online catalogue?
....

c What *can't* you find using the online catalogue?
....

4 🔘60 Listen to the final extract of Robert's introductory tour, and complete the chart.

Borrowing rights

1st year students	N/A
2nd year students	....
3rd year students	....
Academics	....
Research students	....

Did you know …?

Cambridge University Library is one of the biggest in the world. It contains over eight million books, and every year a further 120,000 books and 150,000 periodicals are added to the collection. There are over 100 miles (160 km) of shelves!

Learning tip

Some people naturally speak more quickly than others. When someone speaks quickly, don't panic, listen closely for key words, and check your understanding by asking for clarification.

F Listening – Asking about services

1 Think of some questions you might like to ask when joining a library.

2 🔘**61** Listen and complete each question. Tick ✓ the questions you thought of.

a How exactly do I go about ___searching for a book___ ? ☐
b How do I know .... once I have its location? ☐
c Can I .... on my laptop? ☐
d Can I .... ? ☐
e What if the library doesn't .... ? ☐
f What's the charge for .... ? ☐
g Do staff .... every evening? ☐
h Can I get any help on .... ? ☐

3 🔘**62** Listen to Robert answer each question. Match each question (a–h) to an answer (1–8).

1 _c_   2 ......   3 ......   4 ......
5 ......   6 ......   7 ......   8 ......

4 🔘**62** Now look at the statements below. Write T (true) or F (false) for each statement, then listen again and check your answers.

a You can access the Internet at various locations. _T_
b InterLibrary loans vary in cost depending on your status. ......
c You don't need to pay for the Research Skills programme. ......
d You have to complete a Request form if you want to make copies. ......
e You will need lots of time to get used to the system. ......
f The place to ask for help is called Library Enquiries. ......
g The system of fines for overdue books is quite flexible. ......
h Books should never be left on the desks. ......

Sound smart
Intonation in questions

1 🔘**63** Listen to these questions. Does the speaker's voice go up or down at the end of each one?
a Is it OK to borrow these five books?
b How long can I have them for?
c Do you know how I can get to North Wing 4?
d What time does the library close?

2 Complete the rules using the phrases below.

begin Wh-   *have a Yes/No answer*

Questions that .... usually have rising intonation.
Questions that .... usually have falling intonation.

3 🔘**61** Look again at the questions (a–h) in Section F, Exercise 2. Predict the intonation, then listen and check.

4 🔘**61** Listen and repeat each question. Try to copy the same intonation.

E✗tra practice

Go to the website of a library you know, or try one of the links below. Take a Library Tour! Listen to the audio guide and watch any videos of the services each library offers.

http://www.ncl.ac.uk/library/podcasts/
http://www.library.sunderland.ac.uk/podcasts
http://www.library.jhu.edu/podcasts/index.html
http://www.wku.edu/library/libtour/

Can-do checklist

Tick what you can do.

	Can do	Need more practice
I can talk about my study plans in detail.		
I can ask for opinions and recommendations.		
I can understand detailed course requirements.		
I can ask about and understand a library's services and procedures.		

Unit 16
I work well under pressure

Get ready to listen and speak

- Look at the interview tips. Write *Do* or *Don't* next to each one.

- Now tick ✓ the three *Do's* and two *Don'ts* that you think are the most important.

go to Useful language p. 82

Top interview tips

.... appear interested only in the salary and benefits.

.... appear over-confident or superior.

.... arrive punctually.

.... criticize your current employer or colleagues.

.... dress smartly.

.... look at the wall or floor when you talk.

.... mumble or fail to finish sentences.

.... research the company beforehand.

.... show enthusiasm.

.... tailor your CV to fit the job

Did you know ...?

The first 30 seconds can make or break an interview. Make a good impression by dressing professionally and giving a firm handshake. Look the interviewer straight in the eye, and smile!

A Listening – Getting off to a good start

1 🔘 64 Maria Kelsey is a careers counsellor and expert interview coach. Listen as she gives some advice on giving an effective interview. How many points in the *Top interview tips* does she refer to? ....

2 🔘 65 Now listen as she discusses what to say in an interview. Complete the notes.

- Do not talk about <u>your personal life</u> .
- Talk about any relevant ....
- Mention any .... that relate to the job.
- Mention any skills or .... you have.
- Explain what you .... to the organization.

3 🔘 66 Listen to three candidates in an interview answer the question *Can you tell me a little about yourself?* Look at the notes above and tick ✓ who you think gives the best response.

Juan ☐   Mark ☐   Amelia ☐

4 🔘 66 Listen again and note the good and bad points to each person's response.

Juan   good: <u>talks about qualifications and experience</u>

          bad: ....

Mark   good: ....

          bad: ....

Amelia good: ....

          bad: ....

B Speaking – Beginning an interview

Speaking strategy: Talking about yourself

1 Look at these expressions you can use to talk about yourself and your experience in a job interview.

a As you can see from my CV …
b I graduated in [subject] from [institution]
c I've got a lot of experience in …
d I think I'm good at …
e I'd really like the opportunity to …

2 🔊 **66** Listen again to Juan, Mark and Amelia. Match each person with the expressions they use.

Juan   b   ____
Mark   ____ ____
Amelia ____

Learning tip

If the interviewer asks *Can you tell me about yourself?* or *Could you talk me through your C.V.?*, then talk about your qualifications, skills and abilities and use the opportunity to explain any gaps in your CV. Play to your strengths and try to direct the interview by mentioning the things you want the interviewer to ask about in more detail.

Speak up!

3 Prepare a one-minute answer to the question *Can you tell me a little about yourself?* Make notes.

----

4 Now imagine you are at an interview and give your answer to the question. If possible, record what you say and listen to yourself afterwards. Can you identify any areas you could improve on, e.g. grammar, pronunciation, etc.?

Focus on …
personal qualities and skills

1 Match an expression in A with a similar expression in B.

A	B
1 I work well under pressure.	a I get along well with everyone.
2 I always meet deadlines.	b I like to think of ways round problems.
3 I am a good people person.	c I keep a clear head and never get irritable.
4 I am an excellent communicator.	d I make sure I finish reports on time.
5 I am an effective troubleshooter.	e I am very good at putting opinions across.

2 Write P (positive) or N (negative) next to each personality adjective.

independent [P]   well-organized ☐
opinionated ☐   boastful ☐
strong-minded ☐   domineering ☐
tactful ☐   creative ☐
vain ☐   determined ☐

3 Choose expressions from Exercise 1 and adjectives from Exercise 2 that best describe your personality. Now make a list of your strengths and practise talking about them.

C Listening – Knowing what employers want

1 **67** Listen to Maria Kelsey talk about the skills employers look for. Number each skill area (a–e) in the order she talks about it (1–5).

a Research skills ☐
b Interpersonal skills ☐1
c Problem solving skills ☐
d Leadership skills ☐
e Organizational skills ☐

2 **68** Listen to five questions that employers sometimes ask and match each question (1–5) with a skill (a–e) that it aims to uncover.

1 _e_   2 _____   3 _____   4 _____   5 _____

3 **69** Raj is having a job interview. Listen to him answer each question. Tick ✓ your impression of each answer he gives.

	Good	OK	Poor
1	✓		
2			
3			
4			
5			

4 **69** Listen again to each of Raj's answers and note the reasons for your impression.

1 _____
2 _____
3 _____
4 _____
5 _____

Sound smart
Sounding confident

A confident speaker …
– speaks clearly.
– doesn't speak too fast.
– pauses where appropriate.
– has good pronunciation.
– has a natural stress and rhythm.
– doesn't mumble.
– doesn't hesitate.

1 **70** Listen to three people each answer a different question. Tick ✓ who you think sounds the most confident.
Speaker 1 ☐   Speaker 2 ☐   Speaker 3 ☐

2 **70** Look at the recording script on page 97. Listen again to the most confident speaker. Repeat as closely as you can.

3 Read the three questions the interviewer asks and practise answering each question. Prepare your answer first, then try to sound as confident as you can. If possible, record yourself and then listen to yourself.

Learning tip
If a question is confusing, ask for clarification by saying *I'm sorry I don't quite get your drift* or *What do you mean exactly?* Don't be afraid to pause for a short while if you need time to think.

Did you know …?
It is polite to maintain good eye contact with the interviewer. It shows you are confident and helps to make a good impression.

D Listening – Dealing with difficult questions

1 🔊71 Listen and match each speaker with the question they are answering.

Speaker 1   What do you think is your greatest weakness?
Speaker 2   Tell me about a time you failed badly at something.
Speaker 3   If you like your current job, why do you want to leave?

2 🔊71 Look at these three strategies for dealing with difficult questions. Then listen again and match each speaker (1–3) with the strategy (a–c) that they are using.

a   Show a desire to keep learning and developing. ......
b   Talk about a weakness that is actually a strength. ......
c   Show that you have strategies to deal with the weakness. ......

3 Each speaker answers their question well. How would *you* answer each question?

Learning tip

If an interviewer asks about a weakness or failure, be positive and focus on what you learned from the experience. Say how you would do things differently next time and don't be intimidated. Don't try to cover up mistakes. Always tell the truth!

Class bonus

1 Prepare to role play a job interview. Decide with your partner what the job is and who will be the interviewer/candidate.
   Interviewer: Make a list of questions to ask. You can use the questions in this unit to help you.
   Candidate: Prepare for the interview. Anticipate what questions you may be asked and practise your answers. Use the guidance in this unit to help you.
2 Now role play the interview. When you finish, swap roles.

E✗tra practice

Role play an interview with a friend and record your interview. Then replay the interview and see how well you did. What are your interview strengths and weaknesses? How can you improve your performance?

Can-do checklist

Tick what you can do.

	Can do	Need more practice
I can talk about myself and my strengths.		
I can sound confident and make a good impression.		
I can deal with difficult questions.		

Review 2
Units 7–16

Section 1

🔊 72 **Listen and reply to each statement you hear. Circle your answer.**

1
a I'll show you what I mean.
b I do apologize for the mix up.
c You could try replacing the cartridge.

2
a I don't quite see it like that.
b I'm very sorry for the delay.
c I think we have a bad connection.

3
a Is that correct?
b I completely agree.
c Yes, that's right.

4
a Can I leave a message?
b Do you know when she'll be back?
c I'm sorry, she's out of the office right now.

5
a No, I'm not. That's fine.
b Yes, that's fine.
c That's not really what I meant.

6
a Yes, let's.
b I'll get onto it immediately.
c What exactly are you getting at?

7
a I have no problem with that.
b I'm not sure you've got that right.
c Yes, to show you what I mean…

8
a Yes, of course.
b Right, let's finish there then.
c I'll see what I can do.

9
a I'll put you on hold.
b How are you getting on with that?
c I can come back later.

10
a You could try asking for help.
b I'm not sure I agree.
c That's the way I feel, too.

Section 2

🔊 73 **Read each situation. Then listen and tick ✓ the best reply.**

1 A client complains their order hasn't arrived yet. What do you say?
   a ☐ b ☐ c ☐

2 A colleague's computer doesn't work and you want to suggest a solution. What do you say?
   a ☐ b ☐ c ☐

3 A client asks to speak to your colleague. What do you say?
   a ☐ b ☐ c ☐

4 Sales figures are falling badly. What do you say to your boss?
   a ☐ b ☐ c ☐

5 You are staying in a hotel and phone reception to ask for a late check out. What do you say?
   a ☐ b ☐ c ☐

6 You are listening to a lecture and want the speaker to say more about a certain point. What do you say?
   a ☐ b ☐ c ☐

7 You want to disagree with someone without causing offence. What do you say?
   a ☐ b ☐ c ☐

8 You ask a customer to be patient. What do you say?
   a ☐ b ☐ c ☐

9 You can't hear the person on the phone because a train is passing. What do you say?
   a ☐ b ☐ c ☐

10 You are speaking when someone tries to interrupt. What do you say?
   a ☐ b ☐ c ☐

Section 3

Read each situation and (circle) your answer.

1 Which of the following is *not* a good way to ask for help from a colleague?
   a I could really do with some help to finish this report.
   b Help me finish this report.
   c It would help a lot if you could give me a hand.

2 You want to ask for someone's recommendation. Which expression should you use?
   a Do you think it's worth …ing?
   b I'll get onto it immediately.
   c Could you tell me about that?

3 Which of these expressions should you use to tell a caller someone is unavailable?
   a I'll put you on hold for a moment.
   b I'm sorry she's on another call right now.
   c Who can I say is calling?

4 When listening for the main idea, you should …
   a focus on individual words and phrases.
   b try to take notes of everything.
   c ignore small details and think about the big picture.

5 You want to promise a customer you will take action. What do you say?
   a I'll ask someone to call you.
   b I'll sort it out right away.
   c Please give me a moment.

6 When listening to someone, you should …
   a ask the speaker to repeat if you don't understand.
   b aim to understand almost everything.
   c pretend if you haven't understood.

7 Which is the most polite way to express a disagreement?
   a I think you're wrong.
   b That's not right at all.
   c I'm not sure I agree.

8 When taking notes, you should …
   a only use standard abbreviations.
   b use any abbreviations you wish, including your own.
   c only use abbreviations where necessary.

9 Which of these is *not* a good way to prepare for a telephone conversation?
   a Make a list of points to cover.
   b Have a pen and paper handy.
   c Start eating a sandwich.

10 If the person you want to speak to is not available, what can you say?
   a Do you want her to call back later?
   b Can I take a message?
   c Can you tell her I called?

Section 4

Read each statement and write your reply.

1 Tell me a little about the company you work for, please.
   ----

2 Your hotel room has a shower but you want a room with a bath. You call reception.
   ----

3 What do you think of that suggestion?
   ----

4 You want to remove a stain from your jacket and go into a shop. What do you say to the assistant?
   ----

5 What are your strengths?
   ----

6 You think the latest sales campaign was a complete disaster. Be diplomatic.
   ----

7 You want to introduce the new marketing manager, Mr. Stevens, to your colleagues John and Lizzie.
   ----

8 You need some help to move a large filing cabinet.
   ----

9 Imagine you work in the Accounts department of a large company. Describe your job.
   ----

10 Your boss is on the phone but you need to interrupt to ask an urgent question.

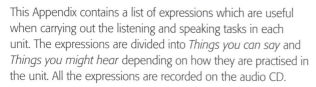

Appendix 1
Useful language

This Appendix contains a list of expressions which are useful when carrying out the listening and speaking tasks in each unit. The expressions are divided into *Things you can say* and *Things you might hear* depending on how they are practised in the unit. All the expressions are recorded on the audio CD.

You can use this Appendix in the following ways.

Before you begin each unit:
1   Look at the expressions and use your dictionary to check the meaning of any words you do not understand.
2   Look at the expressions, but try to work out the meaning of any words you do not understand when you see or hear them in the unit. This is more challenging, but it is a very useful skill to practise.

After you complete each unit:
3   Look at the expressions and check that you understand. Try to think of different examples using the same key words. Find the key words and expressions in the audioscript to see them in context.
4   Listen to the expressions, and notice the stress and rhythm of the speaker. You may want to mark sentence stress in a highlighter pen. Listen again and repeat each expression, practising the stress and rhythm.
5   Listen again to the expressions and notice the pronunciation of any difficult words. You may want to mark word stress in a highlighter pen. Listen once more and repeat each word, practising the word stress.
6   Cover a column, then listen to each expression and repeat from memory. This helps to focus your listening.

Unit 1

Things you can say	Things you might hear
I'm a friend of Tim's.	What did you get up to at the weekend?
Great party, isn't it?	How's work going?
Did you see the news last night?	So, how are the family?
I'm going away on business next week.	It's been hot today, hasn't it?
I'm free tonight.	How long will you be away for?
What's your new place like?	They aren't from here, are they?
How long have you worked there?	We work together in the same department.
They say London is a really fun city.	What a pity!
That's marvellous!	How awful!

Unit 2

Things you can say	Things you might hear
I'm interested in the …	It's got all the latest software.
Can I have a closer look, please?	The picture quality is amazing.
Can you explain what … is?	You can download video games, too.
Sorry, what does hotspot mean?	There's 10% off everything.
What's the battery life like?	All our computers are on sale this week.
I can check email as well, can't I?	It's for people who want to spread the payments.
What is this keypad for?	This one is pretty popular.
What does that button do?	We have a special offer on at the moment.
If you give me a discount, then I'll buy two.	I think we can work something out.
No thanks. I think I'll leave it.	The manufacturer's warranty is a year.
I'll take the extended warranty option.	
I'll pay in full now.	
I'm not sure it's working properly.	
The thing is, it keeps crashing all the time.	

Unit 3

Things you can say	Things you might hear
I'd like to book a check-up, please.	We try to see everyone within two days.
I'm not registered at your practice.	We can fit you in at 4 pm.
I'm here to have a blood test.	You need to fill in this form.
I've had a splitting headache all morning.	Just drop in anytime.
It's killing me.	We do vaccinations as well.
I've had a high temperature for a while now.	We have special clinics for diabetes sufferers.
I feel dizzy and nauseous.	It's all in this leaflet.
I have stomach cramps and diarrhoea.	You have a mild case of the flu.
I can't seem to switch off.	I think you're suffering from depression.
I'm very lethargic.	Take a couple of tablets every four hours or so.
I feel weak and dizzy.	That should get rid of it.
So I need to take two spoonfuls, twice a day?	See me in a month.
So you mean I should finish the course?	

Unit 4

Things you can say	Things you might hear
There's something wrong with this printer.	The car won't start. The battery might be flat.
The air conditioning keeps making a funny noise.	It's not running properly.
Do you know what's wrong with it?	What a drag!
The battery may be dead.	You'd better call the garage quick.
You ought to call a plumber.	It could be the cable.
It won't take five minutes.	It may be the fuse.
The batteries might have run out.	It might be the monitor, I suppose.
It cost a fortune.	It looks like the pump might need replacing.
You really should get this fixed.	I claimed on my household insurance.

Unit 5

Things you can say	Things you might hear
Can I extend my stay if I decide to study longer?	You need to fill out form VAF1.
Sorry, what exactly does 'entry clearance' mean?	Have you got all the supporting documents?
Can you explain what 'Schengen area' means?	You should check you are eligible before you apply.
I need a job to support myself while I'm here.	You need to send the documents by registered mail.
	EAA stands for European Economic Area.
	You need to supply your birth certificate.

Unit 6

Things you can say	Things you might hear
That statue's very impressive.	I'm not really into clubbing.
That's a fantastic view.	That park is handy for joggers.
Is this place famous for anything?	It's popular for walking dogs, too.
I'm starving.	You should definitely go to Fisherman's Wharf.
Is it easy to get around?	You mustn't miss Chinatown.
Where's the best place to go for a night out?	You really ought to visit the museum here.
I like wandering around street markets.	It's hardly ever hot enough to sunbathe.
It's well worth buying a weekly tourist ticket.	The accommodation is quite reasonable.

Unit 7

Things you can say	Things you might hear
I just need to check a few things. I wonder if you could provide …? Could you possibly provide …? I'd be grateful if you could do this for me. I'd appreciate it if you could help me. If possible we'd like to have a late check-out. I need something to put these posters up. Have you got anything for removing stains? Sorry, are you in the middle of something? I could really do with a hand to finish this.	How can I help? Let me just get my booking sheet. OK, fire away! All our rooms are accessible to wheelchair users. These rooms can manage a maximum of fifteen each. I'm sure we can do that for you. I'll see what we can do. How are you getting on with that? I'll get someone to help you out.

Unit 8

Things you can say	Things you might hear
I'm looking forward to working with you. I work for a large finance company. I'm in charge of professional development. I'm responsible for hiring and firing. My main responsibility is to set targets. My job involves taking tough decisions. I manage a group of ten people. I'm interested in research and development. I'm mainly concerned with quality control.	Let me introduce you to the rest of the team. I'd like you to meet our marketing manager. We aim to grow our share of the market. Last year our turnover was in excess of £250 million. We pride ourselves on being at the forefront of technology. Our overriding objective is to deliver quality products. The CEO is in charge of three divisions. The President has control of four divisions.

Unit 9

Things you can say	Things you might hear
I need it urgently. How can we sort this out? Can you post the order special delivery? I think the air conditioning's on the blink again. I can't get this fax to go through. The computer keeps crashing. Have you any idea what this symbol means? You could try pulling that lever. It might be worth changing supplier. Have you tried asking a technician to look at it? You'd like delivery on Friday, is that correct?	Paul speaking. How may I help you? I'm very sorry for the delay. I do apologize for the mix up. Please give me a moment and I'll check. Could you bear with me a moment, please? I'm afraid your order hasn't been processed yet. I'm sorry but there's been an administrative error. I'll get onto it immediately. I'll sort it out right away.

Unit 10

Things you can say	Things you might hear
Would it be possible to speak with Mr Jones, please?	I'm afraid he's in meetings all morning.
Is Joanne there?	She's out of the office at the moment.
Will he be available this afternoon?	He should be available after lunch.
Do you know when she'll be back?	She's on another call at the moment.
Please don't put me on hold.	I'll put you through right away.
Can you ask him to call me?	Sorry, the line's engaged.
Can you say I called?	Would you like to leave a message?
Sorry, can you run that by me again?	I'll make sure he gets the message.
I think we have a bad connection.	

Unit 11

Things you can say	Things you might hear
Let's get down to business, shall we?	Perhaps we can get started.
I'm in favour of it.	The purpose of this meeting is to …
I agree to some extent.	You can see from the agenda that …
I'm not very keen on the idea at all.	How do you feel about that proposal?
I'm not completely opposed to it, but …	Tony, what are your thoughts?
I see your point, but …	Could you please let me finish?
I can see pros and cons each way.	Perhaps we should consider closing the factory down?
I can't agree to that, I'm afraid.	I have no problem with that.
Sorry, can I come in here?	Does anyone have anything else to add?
I'd like to say something if I may.	Shall we move on?
Would it be fair to say that was a mistake?	I think we're drifting off the point.

Unit 12

Things you can say	Things you might hear
Could you explain what you mean by …?	I'd like to begin by …
What exactly are you getting at?	By that, I mean …
Can you go into a bit more detail on …?	So, now I've covered that I'll start with …
Would you expand a little on …?	Basically, what I want to say is …
The talk was about …	I suppose what I'm driving at is …
The speaker began by …	The point I'm trying to make is …
	In other words, what I'm saying is …

Appendix 1 Useful language

Unit 13

Things you can say	Things you might hear
To put it another way …	You can see from this chart that …
In other words …	This graphs shows that …
In short …	What we can see here is …
To sum up, then …	As you can see from …
To show you what I mean …	Let's take a closer look at …
I'd like to draw your attention to …	As you can see from this forecast, …
You'll notice that …	
I've told you about … so let's move on to …	
Now we've looked at … let me turn to …	
The thing to remember here is …	
The crucial point here is …	

Unit 14

Things you can say	Things you might hear
Do you think you could say a bit more about …?	I don't quite see it like that.
I'd like to hear more about …	That's not quite how I see it.
Do you have any specific details about …?	I'm not sure I agree.
Can you give an example of …?	I think you might be mistaken on that point.
In other words, I'd like to know why …	I'm not sure you've got that right.
Basically, what I want to know is …	I don't think you've got that right.
I guess what I'm really asking is …	I think that's a good point.
I agree with some of what you've said …	Sorry, can I finish what I was saying?
That's not really what I meant.	I don't really go along with that.
That's the way I feel, too.	
So, what you're saying is …	

Unit 15

Things you can say	Things you might hear
Next year I intend to study abroad.	It just depends what you fancy.
I plan to go to the US.	Each report will have equal weighting.
My main goal is to improve my English.	We have wireless hotspots dotted around the place.
How exactly do I go about searching for a book?	The fine for overdue books soon mounts up.
What's the charge for overdue books?	
Can I access the Internet on my laptop?	

Unit 16

Things you can say	Things you might hear
I graduated in Hotel Management from …	You should try to play to your strengths.
I think I'm good at working in a team.	Employers look for people who can relate on many levels.
I work well under pressure.	You need to be a good people person.
I'm an effective trouble-shooter.	They want people who can act on their own initiative.
I always meet deadlines.	It shouldn't take you long to get up to speed.

Appendix 2
Pronunciation features

Sound smart

Sound smart gives additional guidance to help you develop your pronunciation skills. You will find ***Sound smart*** activities in most units of this book. This Appendix contains a list of the pronunciation areas covered in ***Sound smart*** at this level.

You can use this Appendix in the following ways:
1 Choose a pronunciation focus you want to practise. Go to the unit where the ***Sound smart*** section appears and practise again.
2 Find a pronunciation focus that you think is especially useful. Practise once more, but this time record yourself and listen afterwards. Try to identify areas you can improve.
3 Practise again, but this time listen to a different recording. Look in the audioscript first to find a suitable recording.

Practise each pronunciation focus in ***Sound smart*** several times. The more you practise, the better your pronunciation will become.

List of pronunciation areas covered in *Sound smart*

Unit 1	Indicating emotion
Unit 2	The schwa /ə/
Unit 3	Using stress to correct misunderstandings
Unit 6	Exaggerating Stress and rhythm
Unit 7	Detecting mood
Unit 8	Word stress
Unit 9	Linking /w/ and /j/
Unit 10	Connected speech
Unit 11	Using stress to emphasize a contrast
Unit 13	Mentioning several points
Unit 14	Sounding polite
Unit 15	Intonation in questions
Unit 16	Sounding confident

Appendix 3
Speaking strategies

Speaking strategies

Speaking strategies are useful techniques to help you communicate in a wide variety of situations. You will find several **Speaking strategies** in each unit of this book. This appendix contains a list of the **Speaking strategies** covered at this level.

You can use this appendix in the following ways:
1. Choose a strategy you want to practise. Go to the unit where the strategy appears and practise again.
2. Find a strategy that you think is especially useful. Practise once more, but this time record yourself and listen afterwards. Try to identify areas you can improve. If possible, practise with an English-speaking friend.

Practise each strategy several times. The more you practise, the easier it will be to use the strategies when you need them in real life.

List of *Speaking strategies* covered

Unit 1	Asking follow-up questions Using question tags Reply questions
Unit 2	Asking how to use something Negotiating Describing a problem
Unit 3	Checking you understand
Unit 4	Speculating about causes Giving strong advice Explaining consequences
Unit 5	Asking for clarification Being concise and to the point
Unit 6	Describing features Making strong recommendations
Unit 7	Making polite requests Explaining what you want Asking for something and justifying reasons
Unit 8	Describing a company Talking about your strengths Describing your job
Unit 9	Dealing with complaints Confirming information Putting forward a solution

Unit 10	Leaving a message Handling incoming calls effectively
Unit 11	Controlling a meeting Being diplomatic
Unit 12	Talking about a lecture Asking for clarification
Unit 13	Describing charts and graphs Linking ideas Giving verbal cues
Unit 14	Disagreeing politely Asking for more detail
Unit 15	Describing plans in detail Asking for opinions and recommendations
Unit 16	Talking about yourself

Appendix 4
Presentation skills

Presentation evaluation

	Excellent		Satisfactory		Weak	

Organization

Were the aims clear?	6	5	4	3	2	1
Were the ideas clearly linked?	6	5	4	3	2	1
Was the summary effective?	6	5	4	3	2	1

Content

Were the facts and information accurate?	6	5	4	3	2	1
Was the content relevant to the topic?	6	5	4	3	2	1
Did the talk hold the audience's attention?	6	5	4	3	2	1
Did the speaker deal with questions effectively?	6	5	4	3	2	1

Language

Was the speaker's language accurate?	6	5	4	3	2	1
Did the speaker use a wide range of vocabulary?	6	5	4	3	2	1
Did the speaker use signposts effectively?	6	5	4	3	2	1

Delivery

Was the speaker's voice clear and easy to understand?	6	5	4	3	2	1
Was the speed and volume appropriate?	6	5	4	3	2	1
Did the speaker emphasize important points well?	6	5	4	3	2	1

Body language

Did the speaker use gestures where appropriate?	6	5	4	3	2	1
Did the speaker maintain good eye contact?	6	5	4	3	2	1
Did the speaker appear relaxed and in control?	6	5	4	3	2	1

Visual aids

Were any visual aids clear and well presented?	6	5	4	3	2	1
Did the speaker exploit the visual aids fully?	6	5	4	3	2	1

What is you overall impression of the talk?   6   5   4   3   2   1

Good points: ....

Weak points: ....

Suggestions for improvement: ....

My performance

	Group's grades	Group's comments
Organization		
Content		
Language		
Delivery		
Body language		
Visual aids		
Overall impression		

My strengths: ....

My weaknesses: ....

Group's suggestions for improvement: ....

Audioscript

These recordings are mostly in standard British English. Where a speaker has a different accent, it is noted in brackets.

 CD1 Social and Travel

Unit 1

2 (d and e = American)
a What did you get up to at the weekend?
b How's work going?
c Did you see the news last night?
d It's been hot today, hasn't it?
e So, how are the family?
f Wow! I like your jacket.

3 (5 = American)
1 Yeah, terrible, wasn't it? I can't believe all the damage that hurricane caused.
2 They're all fine, thanks. Julie, that's my youngest, has just started primary school.
3 Nothing much. I wanted to play tennis on Sunday, but the weather wasn't any good.
4 Thanks! I bought it last Saturday. It was in the sale.
5 Yeah. Great weather for being outside. Shame I had to work all day!
6 It's going well, thanks. I got promoted last month, actually.

4
A
Tim: Hi, I'm Tim.
Kerri: Hi, I'm Kerri. I'm a friend of Michael's.
Tim: Right … Great party.
Kerri: Yes, it is.
Tim: I like the music.
Kerri: Me too.
Tim: I'm in a band, actually.
Kerri: Oh, really?
Tim: Yes, we're quite good. Rock and roll.
Kerri: Hmm, really?
Tim: Yes, we play in pubs and places. I'm free tonight, though. There was a cancellation.
Kerri: I see. Oh, I think I see a friend over there. Nice talking to you, Tim.
Tim: Oh, right. Er yeah. Cheers, then.
B
Nick: Hi, I'm Nick.
Kerri: Hi, I'm Kerri. I'm a friend of Michael's.
Nick: Me too. So, how do you know Michael?
Kerri: We work in the same department.
Tim: Oh, I see. How long have you worked there?
Kerri: Nearly a year.
Tim: Great. Are you enjoying it?
Kerri: It's OK. Every day's different, you know.
Nick: Sounds good. Great party, isn't it?

Kerri: Yeah, it's really good.
Nick: Sorry for asking but … is that an Irish accent?
Kerri: Yes, I come from Dublin originally.
Nick: Do you? That's great. They say it's a really fun city.
Kerri: Yes, it is. Have you ever been to Dublin?
Nick: No, but I've always wanted to go. It's not expensive, is it?
Kerri: Well, prices have been going up …

5 (b and f = Japanese, c, d, e and h = American)
a I have two children.
b I work in London.
c I'm going away on business next week.
d I'm really tired at the moment.
e I saw a great movie last night.
f I really love cooking.
g It's my wedding anniversary next weekend.
h I bought a new computer last month.

6
a Nick: Great party, isn't it?
   Kerri: Yeah, it's really good.
b Kerri: Have you ever been to Dublin?
   Nick: No, but I've always wanted to go. It's not expensive, is it?

7
a A: I bought a new car last month.
   B: Did you? What model did you go for?
b A: I don't like classical music at all.
   B: Don't you? I love it.
c A: I've got terrible backache.
   B: Have you? Oh dear.

8 (a, c and g = American)
a It's my birthday today.
b My car broke down last night.
c I won't be here tomorrow.
d I'm not feeling very well at the moment.
e John's passed his driving test, you know.
f Jane's going on holiday next week.
g This computer doesn't work properly.
h I didn't like that film very much.

9
a Emma: Oh no. It's raining!
   Tony: Great. I was going to play golf this afternoon.
b Julie: It said on the news that property prices are going to fall.
   Frank: Really? That's great. I've just bought a new flat.

10
a
A: Henry. Will you please hurry up? It's nearly half past eight.
B: Sorry. I can't find the car keys.
A: Oh, that's marvellous. Now I'm going to be late for my job interview.
b
A: Is there anything on TV tonight?
B: Not really. Just a black and white film, and I think we've seen it.
A: How exciting. I don't know why we bother having a television.
c
A: I'm full. I don't want dessert, thanks.
B: Oh, what a pity. I'll have to eat this chocolate cake all by myself.

11
a Guess what? I've passed all my exams. That's great.
b There's nothing to do and nothing on TV either.
   That's great.

12
a, b That's really interesting.
c, d How marvellous.
e, f That's exciting.
g, h What a good idea.

Unit 2

13 (b = American; d = South African)
a Customer: So it's got maps of the whole of Europe?
   Assistant: That's right. You can plan your route to wherever you want to go. It's touch screen, too, so it's very easy to use.
b Customer: It's quite light, isn't it?
   Assistant: Yeah. It's very portable. Perfect for carrying around with you on vacation. You can record up to three hours of video onto the hard disk, with audio, and take still pictures too, of course.
   Customer: That sounds great.
c Assistant: This one has a 50-inch screen. The picture quality is amazing, especially if you're watching in high definition.
   Customer: Yeah, I love watching movies so this will be great. I just hope it will fit in my living room!
d Customer: It's wireless, isn't it?
   Assistant: Sure, and it's very light. It has an 80 gigabyte hard disk, and a 3 gigahertz Intel processor, which is really fast. The screen's big, too … 17 inches, and it's got all the latest software of course.

86

Customer: Wow. That's pretty cool.

e Assistant: It can do 24 pages a minute in black and white, and it's a fax, so you can send documents too, if you like.

Customer: Great. And can I make copies as well, yeah?

Assistant: Yeah. Just lift this lid and put what you want to copy in here.

14 (Paola = Italian)

Assistant: Can I help you?

Paola: Yes, please. I'm looking for a smart phone, but erm, I don't know much about them.

Assistant: Right, well with a smart phone you can install software and use it, you know, for your appointments, as an address book for your contacts, that kind of thing… you can take notes and write documents, and link it to your computer and transfer files.

Paola: I see. I'm interested in this one. Is it a good one?

Assistant: This one? Yes, it's pretty popular. It's got all the features you'd expect … a nice screen, a word processor, wireless internet …

Paola: Can you tell me what wireless internet is?

Assistant: Well, it means you can connect to the Internet without have to plug into a computer.

Paola: Right. So I can check my email, can I?

Assistant: Yeah, you can read and send email, and surf the Internet too, as long as you're near a hotspot of course.

Paola: Sorry, what does, erm, 'hotspot' mean?

Assistant: That means an area where you can connect to the Internet.

Paola: Hmm. It's got a camera, hasn't it? Could you tell me about that?

Assistant: Yeah, it's really good. Five megapixels. You can take photos or video.

Paola: And it's got, er, a touch screen. I'd like to know more about that, please.

Assistant: Sure. You just press the feature on the screen you want to use, like this … messages, or whatever … and there you go.

Paola: I see. That's clever.

Assistant: You can download video games, and it's got an MP3 player for your favourite songs. You can even watch TV.

Paola: Wow!

Assistant: Yeah. It's very easy to use.

Paola: Oh, I nearly forgot. What's the battery life like?

Assistant: Not so great, but it comes with two batteries.

Paola: What happens if I press this button here?

Assistant: Er, nothing. You've got to turn it on first!

15

connect   picture   computer

16

camera   popular   feature   address
appointment

17

I often use my phone to surf the Internet.

18

a Can I take a closer look?
b Here's a picture of me and my friend.
c The assistant said there's a sale on today.

19 (The assistant = Australian)

– Can I help you?

a
– Right, well this one is pretty popular.

b
– Sure. Here you are.

c
– That switches it on.

d
– That's for typing messages, like emails and notes.

e
– It switches on the wireless internet connection.

20 (James and the assistant = American)

James: I'd like this DVD recorder, please.

Assistant: Sure. Er, we have a special offer on this at the moment … pay $50 now and then just 20 a month for 12 months.

James: That makes it, what … $290? It only costs 230. That's $60 more.

Assistant: Yes, but it's for people who want to spread the payments, you know.

James: No thanks. I'll pay in full now.

Assistant: Fine. By the way, the manufacturer's warranty is a year, but for an extra 49.99 you can have our three-year instant replacement guarantee. That means if anything goes wrong, just bring it in and we'll exchange it for an equivalent model, no problem.

James: Hmm. No thanks. Oh, I nearly forgot. I don't want to carry this around all day … Do you deliver?

Assistant: Yes, our standard delivery charge is $40.

James: Oh, I see. Er, well … if you give me free delivery, then I'll take the extended warranty option. How's that?

Assistant: Hmm. OK. I think we can work something out here.

21 (Henri = French; Karen = American)

Jane: Hello, I got this for my birthday a couple of months ago but the thing is I never really listen to music. I wonder if I can change it for something else? I haven't even opened it.

Henri: This was a present but the problem is I already have this one. Can I to exchange it,* please, for a different game? I haven't played it.

Pete: Yes, I got this last week but I'm not sure it's working properly. The problem seems to be mechanical – the paper gets stuck all the time. I can't use the fax function, either.

Karen: I've only had this a few months but I don't understand why it keeps crashing all the time when I'm on the Internet, and sometimes when I make a call I can't hear anything. I'd like a refund please.

☞*Did you notice?

Henri says *Can I to exchange it, please?* A native speaker would say *Can I exchange it, please?*

Unit3

22 (a = American; d = Spanish)

a I've had a really splitting headache all morning. It's more like a migraine. Do you have anything for it? It's killing me. What are those, on the shelf behind you …?

b I'd like to make an appointment, please, for as soon as possible. I've had a high temperature for a few days now, and I feel dizzy and nauseous. I need to see a doctor.

c A friend recommended you. I'd like to book a check-up, please, and maybe have a polish, too. I'm not registered here, so what do I need to do?

d Can you please to tell me* which ward Ricardo Suárez is on? He's my father. He was brought in earlier this morning, feeling breathless with a pain in his chest.

☞*Did you notice?

The speaker here says *Can you please to tell me …?* A native speaker would say *Can you please tell me …?*

23

1 I think he's in MIU, that's the Minor Injuries Unit. It's on the fourth floor.

2 These? They're new. They're quite effective. Let me see … you can take two tablets now and another couple in four hours or so. That should get rid of it … They're £4.50.

3 You'll have to come for a new patient check-up before you can be treated. We'll take an X-ray and check your teeth to see what work needs to be done.

4 Right, well we can fit you in at four o'clock this afternoon with Dr Wilson. Is that any good?

24 (Beata = German)

Beata: Hello, I'd like to register as a patient, please? I'm a student from Germany.

Receptionist: Right, well first you need to fill in this registration form. Do you live locally?

Beata: Yes. Just round the corner.

Receptionist: That's all right, then. As you're not a British citizen we need to see your passport, and proof you are working or studying here, so a letter from your school.

Beata: OK.

Audioscript

Receptionist: Once we've looked at your documents and you've filled in your registration form, we give you what's called a database card. You can fill this in at home, with your health details, and details of your family's medical history.

Beata: Oh yes.

Receptionist: Then you can come in for a Well Person Check, which is a basic health check to make sure you're in good shape. Does that sound OK?

25 (Beata = German)

Beata: Oh, and what do I do if I feel sick?

Receptionist: Well, you can either drop in or phone to make an appointment. We try to see everyone within two days. For blood tests, vaccinations and so on you can see the nurse. She's here Monday to Friday, from 8 am to midday. If you are very ill, then we do offer home visits, but you must call before 10.30 in the morning. And if you are sick out of hours, then we have an emergency number you can call. Oh, and if you just want advice, you can phone and speak to the nurse or a doctor between 11.30 and 12 on weekdays. It's all in the leaflet. Erm, what else? Oh, we have a Well Person Clinic on Wednesday and Friday afternoons, where you can get advice on diet, smoking, stress, and blood pressure checks. We also have special clinics for asthma, diabetes sufferers, and a baby clinic for new mothers. Oh yes, and for repeat prescriptions we need 48 hours' notice. Like I say, it's all in the leaflet.

Beata: OK. That's great. Thanks a lot.

26

Anne: I can't seem to switch off. I'm having trouble getting to sleep. I feel really tense and irritable.

Brian: It started a few days ago with a high temperature and now I feel weak and dizzy. I'm very lethargic and I'm shivering and sweating all the time.

27

Anne

Well, I think you're suffering from depression. I'm going to give you a prescription for some Nitropan tablets. They're anti-depressants. Here you are. The tablets I'm giving you are 1000 mg. They're quite strong, so just take one tablet in the morning and another at night. There's enough here for eight weeks, but come back and see me in a month, so we can see how you're getting on.

Brian

I'm afraid you have a mild case of the flu. This is a prescription for some medicine called Cordosole 5 that should sort it out. I want you to take two tablets three times a day, before meals. It should get better in a few days. OK?

28 (Beata = German)

Beata: I feel nauseous all the time. I've been sick a few times and I have stomach cramps and diarrhoea. I feel absolutely awful. I don't know what's wrong with me.

29 (Beata = German)

Doctor: Right, well I think you've got food poisoning.

Beata: Oh, no. Really?

Doctor: Yes, I'm afraid so. But it's not too bad. I'll give you a prescription for some tablets. They're very good. Take two every four hours, and it should sort itself out in a few days.

Beata: OK, so I need to take two tablets every four hours.

Doctor: Yes, and if you're not feeling better in a week, come back and we'll try something else.

Beata: OK. Thank you very much, doctor.

30

a This is a prescription for some medicine that should help sort it out. Take two tablets three times a day, before meals.

b Well, I'm going to give you a prescription. Here you are. Take a couple of spoonfuls of this after every meal.

c Now, these are quite strong, so just take one tablet in the morning and one at night.

d There's enough there for four weeks. Finish the course and then come back and see me if you're not better.

e I'd say it's just a bad case of indigestion. I won't prescribe anything. Just try to eat less and avoid rich food. Oh, and drink plenty of water.

31

A: So you have to take two tablets once a day?

B: No, the doctor said take two tablets **twice** a day.

A: Did you say your left ankle was swollen?

B: No, it's my **right** ankle.

32

a So, your next appointment is on Friday at five thirty?

b Do you have to take two tablets before each meal, then?

c So it's two spoonfuls, twice a day?

d Did you say you had a pain in your left arm?

e You're here to have a check-up, aren't you?

Unit 4

33

[sounds]

34

a (B = Chinese)

A: What's the matter? I thought you'd have left by now.

B: It's the car. It won't start.

A: Oh dear. What a drag. Do you know what's wrong with it?

B: No. I have no idea. When I turn the key nothing happens.

A: The battery may be dead.

B: Hmm. That must be it. I suppose I'll have to call the garage.

A: You'd better call them quick. It's getting late.

B: Oh no. It's nearly six o'clock.

A: Yeah, I know. They might not be open.

b (A = American)

A: There's something wrong with this printer.

B: Really? You've only had it two months.

A: I know, but it won't print anything.

B: It might have run out of paper, I suppose.

A: No. It can't be that. There's plenty of paper. The problem is it just won't print.

B: It could be the cable. Is everything plugged in properly?

A: Yes, I've checked.

B: The cartridge might have run out.

A: Oh yeah. That's a point. I'll have a look.

c (A = Japanese)

A: Hey, what's all this washing doing here? It's soaking wet.

B: I think the washing machine might be broken.

A: Oh no. What's the matter with it?

B: It won't spin, and it's full of water. Look.

A: Oh right. It looks like the pump may need replacing.

B: Maybe. I think I'll take a look inside and find out.

A: You ought to call a plumber.

B: No, no it's not necessary. It won't take five minutes …

35 (The speaker = Canadian)

a Guess what? The dishwasher isn't working again.

b I don't know why, but my radio won't work. I think it's broken.

c My printer won't print anything. Do you know why?

d I've just had a shower but it was freezing cold. I couldn't get any hot water at all.

e There's no picture on the TV. Do you think it's broken?

36 (The speaker = Canadian)

– Is there something wrong with your computer? It could be the cable. It might not be plugged in.

a

– Well, it may be a fuse. One of the fuses could have blown.

b

– It might be the monitor, I suppose. It may not be switched on.

c

– Well, what about the keyboard and mouse? They're wireless, aren't they? The batteries might have run out.

d

– Well, the hard disk might have broken, then.

e

88

37 (a = French; d = Egyptian)
a The toilet doesn't flush properly. I think I'll take a look.
b The cooker doesn't work properly. Maybe I should try to fix it.
c This new DVD recorder might be broken, you know. It won't record anything. Maybe I'll take it back to the shop.
d The air conditioning keeps to make a funny noise*. Do you think I should take a look?
e I've been sick twice this morning. What do you think I should do?

☞*Did you notice?
The speaker here says … *keeps to make a funny noise*. A native speaker would say … *keeps making a funny noise*.

38 (The speaker = American)
– My car isn't running properly again. I'm a bit worried about it.
a
– I know, it's just that last time the repair bill was so expensive.
b
– I suppose you're right. Maybe I'll take a look myself first.
c
– Yes, I guess you're right. But the problem is, I have to be in London tomorrow for an important meeting.
d
– That's a good idea. I'll drop the car off at the garage on my way to the station.
e
– OK. Good idea. Thanks.

39
a I've got really bad toothache.
b I'm tired of doing all this homework.
c I think I eat too much fatty food.
d Oh no. My computer's crashed again.
e I had another argument with my boss yesterday.

40
a Oh, the last emergency I had was last month. I'd been shopping and when I got back to my car I found that someone had smashed the back window and taken all my shopping bags and my handbag … you know, with all my credit cards and money!
b I remember driving back from a friend's house late one night. It must have been around 2 am, and er, they live in the middle of nowhere, so I was driving along this lonely, isolated road … all on my own, and, anyway, my car just stopped … the engine wouldn't work. I was stuck on a lonely road in the middle of the night! And I didn't have any breakdown cover or anything.
c An emergency? Oh, yes. That's easy. A couple of years ago I came back home and found I'd been burgled. Someone had smashed a window and climbed through.

They'd wrecked the place, and taken just about everything of any value.
d Oh, well a few years ago, I remember one day I saw this smoke coming from under the front door of my neighbours' house. There was an old couple living next door, you see, and I thought they might have set fire to something by mistake … left the oven on, or whatever. I knocked but there was no answer …

41
1 I called the police, of course. They came and told me to go through the house and make a list of everything that was missing. None of it was ever recovered, but I claimed on my household insurance so it wasn't a complete disaster. It was very shocking, though.
2 I called the police on my mobile phone and waited for them to arrive. There wasn't much they could do, of course. It was my fault. I should have put my bags in the boot, out of sight.
3 I tried to force open the front door but couldn't. I called 999 and asked for the fire service. Luckily they arrived very quickly and smashed through the door. It turns out my neighbours weren't in, but their TV had somehow caught fire and all the downstairs was covered in black smoke.
4 I called my friend and asked her to come and collect me. We left my car where it was, and the next day I phoned a garage to come and collect it. It cost a fortune, though!

Unit 5

42
Welcome to the UK Visa section. If your enquiry relates to somebody already in the UK, please press 1 now to contact the Immigration and Nationality Directorate of the Home Office. For information about various categories of visa and the visa application process, press 2. If you are enquiring about an appeal, press 3. If you are enquiring about a working permit, press 4. For all other enquiries, or to …

43
Please note you can visit our main website at www.ukvisas.gov.uk for information on the visa application process. You can also download application forms, and email your enquiry. Alternatively, you can send a fax on 020 7008 8359, or you can write to UK Visa section, London SW1A 2AH. If you wish to speak to an operator, you can call us between 9.30 am and 1.30 pm Monday to Friday, except public holidays. To speak to an operator, press 1 now.

44 (Yuki = Japanese)
Visa officer: Hello, UK Visa section. This is Martin speaking. How can I help you?

Yuki: Hello. I'm a Japanese citizen and I'm here as a tourist now but I'm thinking of studying here on a course. Can you tell me if I need a visa?
Visa officer: Will your course be over six months?
Yuki: Yes. I'm thinking of a one-year course.
Visa officer: Then yes, you'll need a Student Visa.
Yuki: Oh, right. What do I need to do to get a visa?
Visa officer: Well, there's quite a few things you need.* First, you need to fill out a form VAF1, and send it in to your local British Embassy Visa section with your passport, two recent colour passport-sized photos and the necessary supporting documents.
Yuki: Sorry, what do you mean by 'supporting documents'?
Visa officer: A letter from the school or college to say what you'll be studying, how long the course is, etc. We also need evidence you can support yourself while you're in the UK, so your last six months' bank statements.
Yuki: I see. And can I work if I have a student visa?
Visa officer: Part-time or holiday work is OK, but you mustn't work over 20 hours a week.
Yuki: OK. Oh, I nearly forget.* How much is it?
Visa officer: A Student Visa is £85.
Yuki: Hmm. How do I apply?
Visa officer: You can apply by post or in person. Just make sure you apply at least one month before you plan to start your studies, but not more than three months.
Yuki: OK. Well, I think that's everything. Thanks very much for your help.
Visa officer: You're welcome. Enjoy the rest of your holiday in the UK.
Yuki: Thanks. Bye.

☞*Did you notice?
The visa officer says *There's quite a few things you need*. This is a common native speaker error. It should be *There are quite a few things you need*.

☞*Did you notice?
Yuki says *I nearly forget*. A native speaker would say *I nearly forgot*.

45
You'll need entry clearance to come to the UK.
a
Entry clearance means official permission to enter the country, so a visa or entry clearance certificate.

If you need extra help you might want to contact the IAS.
b
IAS stands for Immigration Advisory Service. It's an organization which helps people wishing to move to the UK.

You can apply through your nearest UK Mission.
c
That's the local British embassy or consulate in your country.

The UK isn't part of the Schengen area.
d
The Schengen area is a group of EU countries that don't have border or immigration controls.

Are you from an EEA country?
e
EEA stands for European Economic Area. It's made up of the EU countries plus a few others, all in Europe.

🔊 **46** (The speaker = American)
There are three main ways you can get permanent residency, or a green card. If you are coming to work in the US and you have a permanent job, then you can get an employer-based green card. If you have family here who are citizens or already have a green card, then you can apply for a family-based green card. Finally, you can win a green card through the Diversity Visa lottery programme. 50,000 green cards are given away every year to people from countries with low rates of immigration to the US.

🔊 **47**
There are several steps in applying for an employer-based green card. Your US employer must complete Form ETA 750 and the Department of Labor must approve the request. Then, the Department of State must approve an Immigrant Visa Petition, which also has to be sent in by your employer. That's usually Form I-140. After that, you will be given an Immigrant Visa Number.

🔊 **48**
You need to supply your birth certificate, a copy of your passport, and two colour photographs. We also need to take your fingerprints. You should also complete Form G325A with biographical information. We need a letter from your employer, and you have to have a physical. You don't normally need an interview.

🔊 **49** (The official = French)
1
– So, when did you arrive in France?
a
– You have a tourist visa but you now want to work. Why is that?
b
– If we grant you a work permit, it will only be for nine months. How long are you thinking of staying here?
c
– Have you found a job already?
d
– I see. And have you got all the necessary supporting documentation?
e
2 (The official = Canadian)
– You're a student here. What are you studying?
a
– Why do you want to work?
b

– How long are you going to be studying here for?
c
– Have you found a job already?
d
– Have you got a Social Insurance Number?
e

Unit 6

🔊 **50**
Sarah: So what do you think of the view? Not bad, eh?
Paul: Yeah, it's fantastic. You can see for miles. Thanks for showing me round, Sarah.
Sarah: No problem. Glad you're enjoying it!
Paul: What's that over there? That big building with the lights outside?
Sarah: That's Ronelles. It's a good place to go if you want to go dancing. It doesn't close until four.
Paul: Hmm. Well, I'm not really into clubbing.
Sarah: Me neither. Anyway, on the left is Crosswell Hill. I quite often go for a walk there and read a book if the weather's nice.
Paul: Hmm. Crosswell Hill, eh? I guess it's handy for joggers?
Sarah: Yes, and it's popular for walking dogs.
Paul: Well I might go jogging tomorrow morning. Hey, who's that, in the middle? It's huge!
Sarah: People call him Old Keller. It's about 100 feet high, I think. James Keller was an important person here in the last century and when he died they built that. It's made of marble.
Paul: Right. And that's impressive, … on the right, just over there.
Sarah: Yeah, people call that the Typewriter, because it looks like a typewriter. It was built after the Second World War. The names of all the men from the city who died in the war are on it.
Paul: Why are we stopping?
Sarah: Because we're going in there for a bite to eat.
Paul: What … Figo's?
Sarah: Yeah. It's famous for its sandwiches. They're the best in town.
Paul: Great. I'm starving!

🔊 **51**
Sarah: Yeah. It's famous for its sandwiches. They're the best in town.
Paul: Great. I'm starving!

🔊 **52**
I'm starving! We're exhausted! It's fantastic!
It's huge! How terrible! That's fascinating!
I'm furious! I was terrified!

🔊 **53**
a Are you hungry?
b Are you tired?
c That meal was good, wasn't it?
d The kitchen is a bit small.

e That was a bad film, wasn't it?
f I thought it was an interesting programme.
g You look angry.
h That statue's very big.

🔊 **54**
a Is it easy to get to?
b How expensive is it, once you're there?
c What's it like to get around?
d What is there to do?
e Are there any good beaches?
f What's the biggest attraction?
g What's the nightlife like?
h Is it famous for anything in particular?
i Are there any places to visit nearby?
j When's the best time to go?

🔊 **55**
1 Well, the hotels aren't cheap, but if you don't stay in the centre then you can get a good hotel at very reasonable rates, and you can eat out quite cheaply if you know the right places to go. The food is fantastic by the way.
2 The Golden Gate Bridge, for sure. You should definitely walk across it. It's amazing!
3 Er, the old-fashioned Victorian architecture, I guess, and the cable cars, of course. The food is very varied and cosmopolitan, and the views, too, I guess, over the bay area.
4 Loads. There's the bay area, you mustn't miss that. There are lots of parks, great shopping at Union Square. You should definitely go to Fisherman's Wharf, and the sea lions at Pier 39 are well worth a visit. You mustn't miss Chinatown, either. It's the biggest outside China with some great markets. You have to stay there at least five days if you want to see everything.
5 Sure. There are three airports and they're all well connected. You can take the subway system or coach, bus, train. No problem.
6 Yeah. You have to take a day trip to Alcatraz. It's quite expensive, but it's well worth visiting.
7 Well, it's on the coast but it's not really that kind of city. It's hardly ever hot enough to sunbathe or go swimming.
8 Anytime is good, but the warmest days are September and October. It's generally quite mild, so you'll need a coat whenever you go.
9 You should definitely walk, and take a cable car. It's the best way to see the city. Parking's a problem, and anyway you don't really need a car. There are lots of ferries and buses, too.
10 Pretty good. It's not famous for it, though, so you really ought to check what kind of place you want to go to. There are a few good live music bars, I guess.

🔊 **56**
There are three airports and they're all well connected.
It's generally quite mild, so you'll need a coat whenever you go.

57
a The beaches are good but they're very crowded.
b Where's the best place to go for a night out?
c How much is a single room for three nights?
d It's a good place to go if you like wandering round street markets.

Review1

58
Section 1
1 Why are you returning the sweater?
2 Hey, I like your shoes.
3 Oh no. It's raining!
4 My car's making a funny noise.
5 I come from Scotland originally, you know.
6 Are you tired?
7 The thing is, I'm not sure you're eligible.
8 Oh no. My computer's crashed.
9 I don't like travelling by plane at all.
10 Can you recommend a good hotel?

59
Section 2
1
a If you give me free delivery, I'll take the extended warranty.
b Yes, I'd like free delivery, thanks.
c Give me free delivery first.
2
a It might not be broken.
b It can't be the fuse.
c The battery may be dead.
3
a It's famous for a kind of chocolate cake.
b The problem seems to be in the centre.
c Yes, it's great, isn't it?
4
a Is it? That's great.
b You'd better call a plumber.
c What a terrible thing to say!
5
a Yes, I'm interested in that.
b You'd better not do that.
c Sorry. What's a Statutory Waiver Form?
6
a I don't understand why it's stopped working.
b Could you tell me about this model?
c It's stopped working, hasn't it?
7
a You should definitely get to know the area.
b The thing is, I don't really know the area.
c I'd like to know more about the area.
8
a If you give me 10% off, I'll take two.
b I ought to take two.
c You have to give me a 10% discount.
9
a Someone must have repaired it.
b You really should take it to a garage.
c You really should call an electrician.
10
a It can't be a smart phone.
b I'd like to know more about smart phones.
c Is it OK if I have a smart phone?

CD2 Work and Study

Unit7

2
Mark: Hello, The Møller Centre. Mark speaking. How can I help you?
Client: Hello, Mark. It's Natasha Peters here from ARG in London.
Mark: Oh hello, Natasha. How are you?
Client: Oh, I'm fine, thanks. Busy as always. We've got our annual sales conference coming up again and I just need to check a few things.
Mark: OK, well let me just get my booking sheet and … OK, fire away! Dates first, yes?
Client: Yes. It'll be from the 5th to the 9th of July, inclusive.
Mark: So that's five nights. Yes, we can do that.
Client: Great. There'll be 34 this time. That's 19 men and 15 women, plus myself as organizer of course … oh and two senior HR people as well.
Mark: OK … got that. All in single rooms?
Client: Yes … er no. Actually, Sally and James just got married, so I guess they'd want a double. And I'd be grateful if you could give me a double room too please, if possible.
Mark: I'm sure we can do that for you. A bit of extra space is always welcome, isn't it? The HR people might prefer a double each as well.
Client: Oh, yes. Good idea. And one delegate is in a wheelchair, Mr Jackson. He'll need a room on the ground floor.
Mark: Fine. You remember most of our standard single rooms have showers rather than baths?
Client: Yes, but I'd appreciate it if you could give us as many rooms with baths as you can.
Mark: OK. I'll see what we can do. What about training rooms?
Client: This year we need one large training room for us all and then three smaller rooms each holding around a dozen people. Is that possible?
Mark: Hmm … let me see for those dates … Yes, I can give you the Shelley Room in the Study Centre, that seats fifty so you'll all be fine in there, and Meeting Rooms C, E and F. They can manage a maximum of fifteen each.
Client: That sounds perfect.
Mark: It's full-board again, I assume, so breakfast, lunch and dinner each day?
Client: Yes, that's right. Can we have the refreshment breaks at 10.30 and 3.30, please?
Mark: OK, I'll make a note of that.
Client: We need computer data projectors and screens in all the rooms of course.
Mark: No problem. Each room has a whiteboard, flipchart, delegate pads and pencils and water as standard. By the way, we're all wireless now, so delegates will be able to use their laptops for email and so on wherever they want, also at no extra charge.
Client: That's great. And if possible we'd like to have a late check-out on the 10th. Two o'clock, please.

Mark: OK. I'll organize that for you.
Client: Thank you. Now, what's the best price you can do all that for?

3
a (A = Japanese, B = Chinese)
A: I don't know what it's called, but you use it to clean your teeth.
B: A toothbrush? Yes, you can buy one at reception.
b (A = Spanish, B = Chinese)
A: I need something to put these posters on a display board.
B: Sure. Here are some drawing pins.
c (A = Japanese, B = Chinese)
A: Have you got anything for cleaning marks off clothes?
B: Yes, of course. I'll get you some stain remover.

4
Hello. Can I help you?
a
No problem. You can use this hole punch.
Hello. Can I help you?
b
Yes, here's a recharger. Just bring it back when you've finished, will you?
Hello. Can I help you?
c
Sure. Here are some scissors. Watch out! They're quite sharp.
Hello. Can I help you?
d
You mean a calculator. You can borrow mine. Here you are.

5 (Viktor = Russian)
Peter: Oh, sorry Viktor. Are you in the middle of something?
Viktor: No, that's OK, Peter. Come in.
Peter: It's the London project. I could really do with a hand.
Viktor: Really? I thought you were on top of everything.
Peter: Only just. It's a lot more work than I thought when I took it on.
Viktor: Hmm.
Peter: If I had some help, I would be able to finish on time.
Viktor: Well, I don't think we can spare anyone. Everyone's busy on other projects.
Peter: I'm in danger of falling behind. I may not finish on time if I don't get any help.
Viktor: When is the deadline?
Peter: A week on Friday. It would help a lot if someone could write up the report.
Viktor: Hmm. Well, OK. I'll see if I can get anyone to help you out for a couple of days.
Peter: That's great. Thanks a lot.

6
a – d OK, I'll do it for you now.

🔊 **7**

1 Have you finished the report?
2 Do you want a hand with that?
3 Let's do this together, shall we?
4 We need to finish it today.
5 I'll photocopy those files for you, if you like.
6 It's time to start the meeting.
7 Do you think you could help me with this, please?
8 How are you getting on with that?

Unit8

🔊 **8** (Speaker = Australian)

First I'd like to welcome all of you to AGM Industries. As you know, we're fast becoming one of the leading hi-tech companies in the world. Nobody could have foreseen back in 1989 when the company was founded that we would grow so quickly, and so successfully. Today from our home here in Cambridge, AGM Industries controls a multi-million pound business, providing microchip technology to computer manufacturers all around the world. Last year our turnover was in excess of £250 million. We have a total workforce of over 1100 people worldwide, and with your help we aim to grow our 15% share of the market and become even stronger.

🔊 **9** (Speaker = Australian)

At AGM Industries, we pride ourselves on delivering the best products at the most competitive prices … and in the quickest time frame to our customers. I know all of you will take on board these values, and work with me to achieve our goals.

🔊 **10** (Speaker = Australian)

Our company structure here at HQ is fairly traditional. We are headed by the company Chairman, and under him are the President, and the CEO. The CEO is in charge of three divisions; Strategy and Planning, Human Resources and Customer Services. The President has control of four divisions. Operations, which is made up of the Product Management and R and D departments; Technical Services which includes the Quality Control and Technical Support departments … the Business Development division, which includes Sales and Marketing, and finally there is my division, Finance, which stands by itself.

🔊 **11** (The speakers = American)

Peter: Well, this is your office, Lisa. Carol? This is Lisa.
Carol: Hi Lisa. Pleased to meet you. I'm Carol Parks, the Accounts Manager.
Lisa: Hi. Lisa Vickers. I'm looking forward to working with you.
Peter: I'll just show you around, so you get to meet a few more people … Oh, there's Tim. Tim? Let me introduce you to Lisa Vickers. She's our new Accounts Administrator.

Tim: Hello Lisa. I'm Tim Starks, the Payroll Manager.
Peter: Tim's responsible for making sure everyone gets their salary at the end of the month!
Lisa: Ah, so he's a very important person, then!
Peter: Oh, and I want you to meet Helen. Helen Green. She's the CFO. Helen?

🔊 **12** (Michiko = Japanese; Carl = American; Youssry = Kuwaiti; Heidi = German)

Michiko
I'm in charge of promoting the company, both within the industry and in the wider community. My main responsibility is to raise our profile and to make sure the image we project is a positive one.

Carl
Well, my job involves taking tough decisions about our expenditure and any investments we may make. I'm mainly concerned with budget allocation and resource management.

Youssry
I'm interested in people. I'm responsible for hiring and firing, of course, but also for the welfare and professional development of all the staff here.

Heidi
I manage a team of ten people, and together we work to design new technologies that the company can take forward to production. My job involves a great deal of research and study, and also a lot of practical testing and trials.

🔊 **13**

1 analytical
2 creative   flexible   determined
   efficient   reliable   well-organized
   methodical   confident   sociable

Unit9

🔊 **14**

Conversation 1 (B = French)
A: Hello, Life and Times Book Club. Angela speaking. How may I help you?
B: Hello, yes. I still haven't received the book I ordered two weeks ago, I'm afraid.
A: Oh dear. I'm very sorry for the delay.
B: The thing is, I need it urgently.
A: I'm afraid we've been very busy recently and …
B: Can you tell me when will I get it?*
A: Please give me a moment and I'll check … What's your order number?
B: It's, er … GHY723.
A: Right. You ordered *Stress Management* … £14.99.
B: That's right.
A: I can see what's happened. We received your order on the … 23rd, but it hasn't been processed yet. I'll get onto it immediately.
B: You mean you haven't sent it yet?
A: No. Like I say, the order hasn't been processed.
B: But you will send it today, won't you?
A: I can't guarantee it. It's already after three, you see.

B: Is that the best you can do?
A: I'm afraid so. Is there anything else?
B: No, that's all. Thank you.
A: Bye.

↻ *Did you notice
The speaker here says *Can you tell me when will I get it?* A native speaker would say *Can you tell me when I'll get it?*

Conversation 2 (B = Indian)
A: Hello. Home and Office Supplies. Can I help you?
B: Yes, it's Thomson Electronics here. We have an account with you.
A: Oh yes. How can I help?
B: We've just had some printer cartridges delivered but they're the wrong ones. They don't fit.
A: Oh dear. I do apologize for the mix-up.
B: I don't know how you could've got it wrong. We order from you all the time.
A: I know, but unfortunately we've been having computer problems.
B: Well, how can we sort this out?
A: Could you bear with me a moment, please? … Ah yes, I have the order here. You want 25 HP356 printer cartridges. Is that correct?
B: Yes, that's right. But you've sent us 25 HP56 cartridges instead.
A: I see. I'll sort it out right away and we'll post the order special delivery.
B: Thanks.
A: I'll put a £30 credit on your account to make up for the inconvenience, as well. Is that all right?
B: Oh, that's very nice. Thanks.
A: Not at all. It was our mistake. Can I help you with anything else?
B: No thanks. That's it. Bye.
A: Goodbye.

🔊 **15** (d = Chinese)

a I asked for a brochure a month ago, but I haven't received one yet.
b I placed an order with you over a month ago, but I haven't received anything yet.
c I've been trying to order online, but it won't accept payment.
d You seem to have charged me twice for the same thing on the latest invoice.
e The manager said he would call me back today, but I've heard nothing.

🔊 **16** (a and e = Chinese)

a I ordered a set of six wine glasses, but when they arrived three were broken.
b The TV I bought from you has stopped working. I've only had it two months.
c I'm sorry, but you seem to have delivered the wrong sofa. I ordered a blue one and this is black.
d I've just seen my bank statement, and I've been charged the full price for the DVD recorder I bought, but it was 15% off.
e I've been trying to get through to your technical support line for ages, but it's constantly engaged.

🔊 **17**
– I paid for a Canon X40 printer online, but you've just sent me an email saying it's not in stock.
a
– Well, I need one urgently. When will you have more in stock?
b
– Well, can you make sure you send me one as soon as they come in? My name's Ketson. It's order number 2374.
c
– OK, thanks a lot. Bye.

🔊 **18**
a What would you like to order?
b We can guarantee delivery by the end of the month.

🔊 **19**
a I asked you over a month ago for a brochure.
b Please give me a moment to check.
c I'll get onto it immediately.
d We'll post the order special delivery.
e I'll post it in the afternoon.
f Can I ask who is speaking, please?
g I do apologize for all the inconvenience.
h You sent me an email to ask about delivery.
i I'll be out of the office all next week.

🔊 **20**
1 This camera won't record anything. I can't understand it.
2 This computer keeps crashing. It's really annoying.
3 The projector doesn't work. I turn it on and nothing happens.
4 It's really hot in here. I think the air-conditioning's on the blink again.
5 This printer won't print anything.
6 I can't get this fax to go through. It won't send it.

🔊 **21**
1 You've checked there's some paper in it, haven't you?
2 Yeah. It's probably the thermostat again. I'll call Maintenance.
3 The battery might be low I suppose. I'll get you another one.
4 Why don't you ask David? He's good with computers.
5 The bulb might have gone. Do you want me to call the technician?
6 It might be worth checking the number. Are you sure it's right?

🔊 **22** (Pilar = Brazilian; Martin = American)
Martin: Pilar. There's something wrong with this photocopier. I keep pressing the button but it won't do anything.
Pilar: Oh dear. Do you want me to give you a hand, Martin?
Martin: Thanks. Have you any idea what this symbol means? The one flashing here.

Pilar: Maybe it means there is some paper stuck inside. It might be worth opening it and having a look.
Martin: How do I do that?
Pilar: You could try pulling that lever there. That's the one.
Martin: Oh yes. You're right. There is some paper stuck in here. Thanks a lot. I think that's sorted it now.

🔊 **23**
a We've got so many orders we're in danger of falling behind on deliveries.
b My computer's running really slow. It's so annoying!
c Our main competitors are all cheaper than we are.
d I'm not sure how we can get clients to buy any more of our stock.
e I've had reports that staff morale is rather low.
f That's the third time this week our electricity supply has been disrupted.

Unit 10

🔊 **24** (A = American)
Conversation 1
A: Hello, Smart Finance Limited.
B: Hello. This is Norman Silvers from Highgate Investments. Would it be possible to speak to Mr Fredericks, please?
A: I'm afraid he's in meetings all morning.
B: I see. Will he be available this afternoon?
A: Yes. He should be free after lunch.
B: Could you ask him to call me? It's very important.
A: Certainly. Norman Silvers, wasn't it?
B: Yes, from Highgate Investments. He has my contact details.
A: Very good. I'll make sure he gets the message.
B: Thanks very much. Goodbye.

Conversation 2
A: Hello, Accounts.
B: Hi, it's Charlie. I need to check some figures from the sales report. Is Sharon there?
A: Nope. She's out of the office at the moment.
B: Do you know when she'll be back?
A: No, I'm afraid not.
B: Well, when she gets in can you say I called?
A: Sure. No problem.
B: Thanks a lot. Bye.

🔊 **25** (The speaker = Australian)
– Hello, Richmond Travel Ltd.
a
– I'm afraid she's in meetings all morning.
b
– Yes. She should be free after lunch.
c
– Certainly. What was your name again?
d
– Very good. I'll make sure she gets the message.
e
– Goodbye.

🔊 **26**
– Hello, Personnel.
a
– Nope. She's out of the office at the moment.
b
– She should be in after two, I think.
c
– Sure. No problem.
d
– 344. OK, got it.
e
– Bye.

🔊 **27**
Conversation 1 (Tim = Canadian)
Tim: Hello, Tim speaking.
Judy: Hi, Tim. It's Judy. Is Mike there?
Tim: Hang on. I'll try his office for you. … No, sorry. The line's engaged.
Judy: Oh, right.
Tim: Can I take a message?
Judy: No, it's OK. I'll call back later.

Conversation 2 (Hugo = Spanish)
Jane: Hello. This is Jane Garston.
Hugo: Hello. I'd like to speak to Brian Cardew, please.
Jane: I'll just put you through … I'm afraid he's on another call right now.
Hugo: Oh, well, um …
Jane: Would you like to leave a message?
Hugo: No, that's fine. I send him an email.*
Jane: OK. Thanks for calling.

↻ ***Did you notice?***
Hugo says *I send him an email.* A native speaker would probably say *I'll send him an email.*

🔊 **28** (The speaker = French)
– Oh, hello. I'd like to speak to Françoise Chirac, please.
a
– Thank you.
b
– Oh, I see.
c
– Yes, please. Could you ask her to call me as soon as possible?
d
– Pierre Dupont. Françoise has my contact details.
e
– Thank you. Goodbye.

🔊 **29**
– Hi, Nigel. It's Samantha. Is George there?
a
– Thanks.
b
– Oh, right.
c
– Yes, please. Can you tell him I called?
d
– Yes, that's right.
e
– Thanks. Bye.

🔘30
a Do you know when she'll be back?
b Would you like to leave a message?
c Could you tell her I called?
d Do you want to call back later?
e When's the meeting going to finish?

🔘31
a What do you want to talk about in the meeting?
b Can you tell me if you're going to leave early?
c When would you like to have the meeting?
d When could you give me an answer?
e When do you expect to get a promotion?

🔘32 (b = Kuwaiti; e = Chinese)
a Hello. I'd like to speak to Mr Watson in the Personnel Department please about the position advertised in the local paper. If you …
b My name? Yes of course. It's Hashem Aghajari. I'm calling about …
c So we definitely need this order by the 6th …
d The thing I want to … stress is … that the delivery should be … made … on the 20th at the latest …
e So that means all five of us need to be there on the fourth by three or at the latest four or else the meeting about ZX34 transit plans in Room 21 will have to relocate to my office on the seventh floor which is available until six … Got it?

🔘33
a Would you mind spelling that for me?
b Sorry. Can you run that by me again?
c Could you speak up, please?
d I think we have a bad connection. I'll call you back.
e Could you speak a little slower, please?

🔘34
a I'm sorry, I think I pressed the wrong extension. Can you put me through to …
b Peter called earlier. He's trying to get some figures together and he wants you to see him at five o'clock in his office if possible …
c If Mr Banks calls, then tell him I'm in a meeting will you, and after you've typed up the Vicks report this morning, I'd like you to first arrange a meeting with Mike at FedEx for sometime next week, and then book a flight to New York leaving before midday tomorrow.
d Please tell her that Machiko Katsumata called.
e If Mrs Henries calls … most important … don't agree until … meet first … 10th at the earliest …

Unit 11

🔘35
OK, everyone? Erm … Perhaps we can get started. We have a lot to get through over the next couple of days. First, let me thank you all for coming. I know some of you have travelled a long way. I'd especially like to welcome Javier and Ian who've come from Spain to be here, and Inessa for interrupting her holiday. As you know, the purpose of this meeting is to come up with some recommendations for turning things around in the light of appalling sales figures for the last quarter. You can see from the agenda that we have several items to cover. Namely, falling European sales, increased competition in our domestic market …

🔘36 (Javier = Spanish)
David: So, I'd like to know what everyone thinks about the Board's proposal to pull out of France and Germany? How do you feel about it, Inessa?
Inessa: Well, David, I think it's a bold move and it's probably the way we need to go, so yes, I'm in favour of it.
David: Hmm. Javier, what are your thoughts?
Javier: I agree to some extent, but there are considerable costs involved. For example …
Ian: Sorry, can I come in here?
David: Could you let Javier finish, please Ian? Javier, you were saying?
Javier: Yes, thanks. The costs are huge. It will cost over five million just to close our branches there and we can't guarantee the move will succeed. It's risk.* I'm not completely opposed to it but, er, you know …
David: Ian, you wanted to say something?
Ian: Yes, Javier I see your point, but, well, basically I'm not very keen on the idea at all. As well as the costs, we need to consider our long term future. We need to expand our European operations, not close them down!
Inessa: Perhaps we should consider just closing down the least profitable of our branches in France and Germany.
Javier: I have no problem with that. What do you think, David?
David: Well, I can see pros and cons each way. It's quite a mixed picture.
Ian: I can't agree to that, I'm afraid. Like I say, I think we need to stay in France and Germany. That's where our future lies.
David: Right. Does anyone have anything else to add? OK, then. I think I need to pass all your thoughts on to the Board for further review. Clearly, we can't come to a unanimous decision here. Now, shall we move on?

☞**Did you notice?**
Javier says *It's risk.* A native speaker would probably say *It's a risk* or *It's risky.*

🔘37
We need to expand our European operations, not close them down!

🔘38
a Sales should be increasing, not falling.
b We need our staff to work longer hours, not shorter.
c We should be hiring staff, not firing them.
d We need more skilled labour, not unskilled labour.
e We need to be more competitive, not more expensive.

Unit 12

🔘39 (The speaker = American)
Now, I'd like to begin by giving you a few pointers on taking notes in lectures. This is a vital skill, so listen up! Most important of all is that you shouldn't try to make a note of everything you hear. A lecture is not a dictation. You have to listen and decide what *is* important and what *isn't*. Second, when you make notes, don't write everything in full. Use abbreviations, symbols, numbers … anything to help keep pace. Also, try to organize your notes effectively. Furthermore, you should try to be an active listener. By that, I mean you need to try and predict what the speaker is going to say … so before the lecture ask yourself what you already know about the topic, and during the lecture think about where the talk might be heading. Another useful tip is if you miss something then don't panic. Lecturers usually repeat themselves … certainly, the important information … for example by paraphrasing or in summary. Something else you should be sure to do is listen for the main ideas, as well as the details, otherwise you won't be able to see the wood for the trees. And finally, after the lecture, you should review your notes as soon as possible. That means basically writing them out again, but this time reorganize them, highlight the main points, and even add your own thoughts and comments in the margin. Reviewing your notes in this way will help everything sink in, and make a useful study aid. So, now I've covered that I'll start with the register.

🔘40
Now, most people would agree that the massive economic growth China has enjoyed in the last forty years represents perhaps the most significant geopolitical event of the 21st century. It started with the economic reforms back in the late 1970s, before which time China's economy was largely rural.

Since the 1970s China's economy has grown on average 10% a year. Exports have soared and industrial production is growing at 17% per annum. Since 2001, China has doubled its share of global manufacturing output. In fact, China is second only to the US, and most forecasts suggest it will overtake the American economy within the next ten years.

China's population of 1.3 billion makes it a staggering one fifth of the world's population. This huge population resource means not only is China the world's largest market, but it also underpins the main reason for its economic rise – a large workforce. The incredible economic growth in China has meant huge changes for the workforce. For example, it is estimated that about 200 million people have moved from rural areas to urban areas to find work, resulting in the biggest mass migration in history. Employment in agriculture has been replaced for millions by jobs in manufacturing and industry, which, for many people, has meant having to retrain, acquire new skills, and adapt to a new way of life. Many would argue that the growing middle class is the backbone of China's success.

However, some economists see weaknesses in China's economy. They point, for example, to the fact that many of the manufacturing companies that produce goods in China are in fact foreign. These foreign companies, they argue, will continue to invest in China while labour costs are low, but if wages start to rise too much, they may move their production to other parts of the world where rates of pay have remained lower.

China has come a long way since the 1970s, but it would seem that, for China to continue its economic success story, the country must not rely on outside investment and expertise, but must invest more in skills and training in order to produce its own experts and entrepreneurs of the future.

🔘 41
a (The speaker = Indian)
The talk was about China's economy. The speaker began by talking about the emergence of China as a major economic power, which started with economic reforms in the late 1970s. Then she gave some statistics about China's economy today. It's the second largest in the world, and should overtake the US in a few years. She went on to talk about China's huge population, and how large numbers of people have moved from rural to urban areas to find work. Then she mentioned some potential weaknesses in the Chinese economy, such as a dependence on foreign companies. Finally, she talked about the challenges for the future, especially the need for China to invest more in skills and training.

b
The talk was about the growth of China's economy. The speaker began by saying it was the most significant event of the 21st Century, growing 10% a year although it's still not the biggest economy. After that she said that millions of people in rural areas had moved from the countryside to the city, and this was the biggest mass migration in history, which I thought was amazing. I think she said something about

wages going up there, but basically her idea is that the Chinese economy will continue to grow.

🔘 42
a Could you explain what you mean by the biggest mass migration in history?
b Can you go into a bit more detail on the cost of labour in China?
c What exactly are you getting at when you refer to the middle class as the 'backbone of China's success'?
d Would you expand a little on the impact of China's economic growth?

🔘 43
1 Basically, what I want to say is that the purchasing power of this new class is helping to support the domestic economy.
2 I suppose what I'm driving at is that never before has such a huge movement of people from rural to urban areas taken place over such a short period of time.
3 Yes, an average factory worker in a coastal city in China earns up to $350 a month these days, while in some other countries it can be as low as $100. The point I'm trying to make is that rising wage costs could make China less attractive for foreign companies.
4 Well, I think it's a necessary factor for global economic development. In other words, what I'm saying is that without China as the economic powerhouse in the world, all our economies would be worse off.

Unit 13

🔘 44 (Kirsty = New Zealand)
So, let's consider where we expect to see visitors coming from in 2012. You can see from this chart that we anticipate the vast majority of our visitors to continue to come from our neighbour Australia. Other significant markets are the UK which we have included along with Nordic countries and Ireland, North-East Asia, principally Japan, and the Americas, notably the US of course.
Let's take a closer look at our biggest market by far, Australia. This graph shows that visitor numbers from Australia will continue to rise. Growth here will remain steady, as it has been for the last twenty and more years. We expect this to continue, thanks to a combination of low airfares and aggressive marketing by our Ministry of Tourism in Australia. With total growth around 3% per annum we expect numbers from Australia will get up to around 1.2 million.
As for why people come here, we don't expect that to fluctuate much at all. What we can see here is that we expect almost no change in fact, with the top reason continuing to remain holiday, where it's mainly sightseeing and outdoor activities that are of interest, and then the principal other reasons … visiting friends and relatives and business.

🔘 45
People come to New Zealand to go sightseeing, do outdoor activities and go shopping.

🔘 46
a Great Britain is made up of three countries: England, Scotland and Wales.
b Wales is popular for walking, its great beaches and its many castles.
c In Scotland tourists visit Edinburgh, Loch Ness and enjoy the great scenery.
d Popular tourist destinations in England are the Lake District, Cornwall and of course London.
e London's top attractions include the London Eye, the Tower of London and Buckingham Palace.
f Three popular museums are the National Gallery, the British Museum and the Tate Modern.

🔘 47 (Speaker = Chinese)
a In fact, the weather was unusually hot for the whole of the summer and as a result icecream sales increased sharply.
b Demand all over the country rose to new heights. For example, in London we sold 35% more ice cream than last year.
c Of course, all this has had a tremendous effect on our bottom line and has helped to lift us out of the difficult situation we were facing last year. In other words, we no longer have to consider a programme of compulsory redundancies.
d … and that is basically all I have to say for the moment. To sum up then, results have far exceeded our expectations and the future for Mills Ice cream looks very bright indeed.

Unit 14

🔘 48 (E = Italian)
A: According to the UNESCO report we read, there are more than 6,000 languages in the world today, but over half are in danger of dying out before the end of this century …
B: Yeah, like the language used by the Ainu in Japan. It has less than a few hundred speakers left.*
A: Or the Maori language in New Zealand. The report says one language becomes extinct every two weeks. It's terrible. Basically, I think we need to do whatever it takes to keep these languages alive.
D: Hmm. I don't quite see it like that. Can you actually protect a language anyway?
B: Yes, Welsh is a great example.
D: Really?
B: Yes. When the Welsh Language Board was set up in 1991, only 19% of the population spoke Welsh. Now it's up to around 25% I think, and rising, and most speakers are younger than 30.
A: Yeah, the fact is language revitalization is critical. Every government should do what they can to support languages.

D: I'm not sure I agree. I wonder if we need 6,000 languages. I mean, languages become extinct for a reason, you know … because nobody wants to speak them! We can't assume that every language must naturally survive.

E: I think that's a good point. I mean, things change.

C: But, you know, languages tell us about who we are. You can't separate language from culture. Take one away, and the other dies.

E: I don't agree. At least, not for Italy.

A: Do you think you could say a bit more about that, please Maria?

E: Sure. Before, there have been over a hundred languages* or at least different dialects, in Italy but now basically we all speak Italian, we all feel Italian. We haven't lost our culture because we all speak the same language.

D: And if we all spoke the same language at least we'd understand each other. There'd be fewer wars and …

C: I think you might be mistaken on that point. I don't think there would be fewer wars, for a start.

E: Also it costs millions and millions of pounds to keep these tiny languages from dying out.

A: I don't think you've got that right.

C: So you think everyone in the world should speak English?

E: Why not? *We* all do! Let's use the money on food and clean water for people.

B: That's ridiculous.

D: I don't think so. Are you saying we should let people die just to spend the money on saving a language hardly anyone speaks? Which is more important … the life of a person, or the life of a language?

☞*Did you notice?

The native speaker here says *It has less than a few hundred speakers left*. It should really be *It has fewer than a hundred speakers left*. This is a common occurence in everyday speech.

☞*Did you notice?

Speaker E says *Before, there have been over a hundred languages*. A native speaker would say *Before there were over a hundred languages*.

🔘49

a English is the most widely-spoken language in the world.
b I heard the earliest writing is from China around 2,000 years ago.
c About a quarter of all languages are African languages.
d Japanese is traditionally written from top to bottom, and left to right.
e Greek is the oldest language spoken in Europe today.
f People in Brazil speak Brazilian.

🔘50

a English is a really difficult language to learn.
b I think children learn languages more quickly than adults.
c We need to protect all endangered languages.
d The world would be better if we all spoke the same language.
e Language and culture are not related.
f I think fewer people are learning English these days.

🔘51

A/B I think you might be mistaken on that point.

🔘52

A/B I'm not sure you've got that right.
A/B That's not quite how I see it.
A/B I'm not sure I agree.
A/B Sorry, can I finish what I was saying?

🔘53

1 In other words, I'd like to know why you think English has become so important.
2 Basically, what I want to know is why more people don't care about the problem.
3 I guess what I'm really asking is do you think another language will ever take over as the language of global communication?
4 To put it another way, are some languages more important than others?
5 I suppose what I'm driving at is can we really protect all the languages there are in the world today?

🔘54

a Sorry, what do you mean exactly?
b I agree with some of what you've said.
c No, sorry. I don't really go along with that.
d I really do think that it's important.
e That's the way I feel too.
f Can we get back to the point here, please?
g My mistake. I got it wrong. Sorry.
h That's not really what I meant.
i OK. So what you're saying is …
j What do you think, Peter?
k Sorry, can I just finish what I was saying?
l Can I say something here?

Unit 15

🔘55 (Stefania = Italian; Habib = Saudi Arabian)
Stefania
I plan to go to Beijing for a year if I can afford it and stay with a host family while I'm there. My main goal is to improve my Chinese. I've been studying at college here for three years but I expect actually living there will, you know, help me a lot. When I will come back to Italy* my experience and language skills will help me get a good job, perhaps in an import–export agency.

Habib
Well, next year I intend to start business studies course* at college here in Riyadh. The course is two years so I hope it'll help me to get a good job after I graduate. That's the main purpose in fact. But also I hope to develop contacts in international business, and English is a big part of the course so that's another benefit.

☞*Did you notice?
Stefania says *When I will come back* … A native speaker would say *When I come back*.

☞*Did you notice?
Habib says *I intend to start business studies course*. A native speaker would say *I intend to start a business studies course*.

🔘56

– Yes, do you want to ask me something?
a
– That sounds like a good idea.
b
– Well, longer is better I suppose. Two months, if possible.
c
– Either of those places would be fine. It depends if you want to go to a big or a small city.
d
– A host family would give you more opportunities to practise your English and learn about British culture, and it's probably cheaper.
e
– Study full-time if you can. But make sure you get the chance to socialize, too.
f
– Exams can be useful, but I think General English is best at this stage.
g
– Sure. They're different, of course. The accent is different and everything. It just depends what you fancy, really.

🔘57 (The professor = American)
OK, so the focus of this semester will be on the development of the EU and its enlargement. You'll have four written assignments to do. These must be typed and handed in on time or they will not be considered. They have equal weighting and make up 20% of your final grade, so take them seriously. We'll also have a couple of exams; a mid-term exam which will count 30% towards the final grade and an end of term exam which will also count for 30%. Each exam will be in two parts, a multiple choice test and then four short essay questions. At the end of the semester you'll also have to give an oral report, which will take the form of a 15 minute presentation on a topic of your choice related to the main course themes, followed by a Q and A session also of 15 minutes. This will comprise 10% of the final grade. The remainder will be at my discretion depending on how well prepared

you are for each class, and also how much you participate in each class. Attendance is also a factor in that there are 23 classes this semester and you need to attend at least 80% in order to pass. So that means if you miss more than four classes, you fail. I hope you all understand that. The grade you get is not dependent on other students in the class, so it is possible for everyone in the class to get As or to get Fs. To get an A you need above 90%, 80–90 is a B and 70–80 is a C. D is 60–70 and below that is a fail, F. Basically, if you put in the time and effort needed you will pass.

🔊 **58**

OK, so if you'll all follow me … Opening hours are nine to seven Monday to Friday, and nine to five on Saturday, during term time. Out of term we open from ten till one weekdays only. Oh, and if you turn up less than fifteen minutes before closing, you can't come in.

🔊 **59**

Over there is the Reading Room. That's where you can access materials that can't be taken out, so, er, articles, journals and so on. Rare books and manuscripts are in the North Wing, over there… also for reference only of course. To search for a book, you'll find our main catalogue here in the Green Room, or you can search online if you have a password and what you want was published after 1978. For any special collections you need to come in and go through the supplementary catalogues in the South Wing.

🔊 **60**

First and second year students can't borrow books. Third year students can borrow a maximum of five books for up to eight weeks, and if you're an academic or research student you can borrow ten books for up to eight weeks. All books to be taken out at Lending Services in the lobby. OK, any questions?

🔊 **61**

a How exactly do I go about searching for a book?
b How do I know where to find a book once I have its location?
c Can I access the Internet on my laptop?
d Can I make copies?
e What if the library doesn't have the book I want?
f What's the charge for overdue books?
g Do staff clear away books every evening?
h Can I get any help on using the library?

🔊 **62**

1 Yes, we have wireless hotspots dotted around the place … just look out for the Wi-Fi symbol.
2 Then you can make an InterLibrary loan and we'll order it from somewhere that has it. It costs five pounds for members of the University and ten pounds for everyone else.

3 Sure, just ask at Library Services. We also run a Research Skills programme. It's free, so all you have to do is sign up!
4 Yes, the copy room is on the fifth floor. If it's a journal and you need permission, then fill out a Request form and they'll do everything for you. It takes 24 hours.
5 Just follow the system we use. Each book is numbered with the floor and row, and has a code to show which part of the library it's in. You'll soon get used to it.
6 Start by looking in the main catalogue and then if it's not there, you can go to Library Services desk and they'll help you find what you're looking for.
7 Twenty-five pence a day. It soon mounts up, especially if you have several books, and we make virtually no exceptions unless you have a very good excuse so you have …
8 Yes, but if you put a Retainer slip inside, you can leave books you haven't finished with on the desk you're using and the staff won't clear them away.

🔊 **63**

a Is it OK to borrow these five books?
b How long can I have them for?
c Do you know how I can get to North Wing 4?
d What time does the library close?

Unit 16

🔊 **64** (Maria = American)
Basically, it's all about preparation. Make sure you know all about the company, and check your resumé matches the job you're applying for. Then on the day wear something smart, get there on time, and when it's your time to shine, get in there and give it all you've got. You must appear like you really want the job. Don't act like you know it all, though. That won't go down well.

🔊 **65** (Maria = American)
Now, employers often start off with a question like *Can you tell me a little about yourself?*, to get things going and what a lot of people do, believe it or not, is they talk about their personal life. You know, their kids, what food they like and goodness knows what. That's bad. Do not talk about your personal life. Basically, you should talk about any relevant work experience. That's what employers want to hear. Play to your strengths, and mention any qualifications that relate to the job. Anything at all, you know, as long as there is a clear link with the job you are applying for. You should mention any skills or special training you have, as well, and perhaps above all what employers want is to know how *you* can help them, so explain what *you* can bring to the organization.

🔊 **66** (Juan = Spanish; Amelia = Italian)
Juan: I graduated in Accounting from Madrid University and after I graduated I started work as a Junior Accountant at MTW. Now I am still

there, and I am head of my department so I'm used to managing people and I have got a lot of experience in implementing financial programmes. I enjoy cycling and going to the movies, and I am married with three kids. I would like to work here because you are the best company in the business.
Mark: As you can see from my CV, I attended Manchester International University and studied Marketing for three years. Then I moved to Richmond in the States and took my MBA. That really helped me gain a better understanding of marketing strategies and how to use them effectively. Since then I've worked as Strategic Marketing Manager for Gaviso. I'd really like the opportunity to use all this experience here as Marketing Director. I have a lot of ideas that I'm sure will be very effective in marketing your products to a wider audience.
Amelia: Well, I'm quite easy-going I suppose. I can work well with anyone. I have a good education. My degree is from the Sorbonne in Paris. It's a very good university. I like a challenge too, in my work and my personal life. I plan to climb Mount Everest one day. I'm freelance now but in my last job I had a lot of responsibility, a lot of budgets and things. In my spare time I read and go walking. I enjoy my work and I think I'm good at my job, so, yeah, what else can I say?

🔊 **67** (Maria = American)
Well, employers look for people who can relate on many levels, you know. People who can talk to the President of the company or the worker on the shop floor. They want someone who is a good people person, basically. They also value the ability to take charge and head things up from the front when it matters. Of course, they need people who are good planners, efficient types, you know … although increasingly these days they also want free-thinkers who can work their way through difficulties. Oh, and employers want people who can act on their own initiative to collect whatever information they need, rather than sit around scratching their heads wondering what to do!

🔊 **68**

1 Do you manage your time well?
2 What's the biggest difficulty you have ever faced at work?
3 Can you remember a time when you helped resolve a conflict among your colleagues or classmates?
4 Have you ever had to work on a topic you knew nothing about?
5 Are you comfortable making decisions and taking the lead?

🔊 **69** (Raj = Indian)
1 Interviewer: Do you manage your time well?
    Raj: Yes, I think so. I'm a very organized person. I have a huge filing system and

b

I always know where everything is. I schedule my day carefully and try to make appointments I can keep.

2 Interviewer: What's the biggest difficulty you have ever faced at work?

Raj: Last year we had a problem with some new software we'd installed. It wasn't working properly and we were losing a lot of money because of it. It was down to me to fix it so I worked round the clock. I finally found a way round it, but it was really hard work and the pressure was unbelievable!

3 Interviewer: Can you remember a time when you helped resolve a conflict among your colleagues or classmates?

Raj: A couple of months ago there was a problem in my department. A new system meant that you had to sign in and out all the time. Many people didn't like this because there was only one place you could sign in, which was a long way from where most people work. I suggested we put signing-in stations at several locations, and that seemed to solve the problem.

4 Interviewer: Have you ever had to work on a topic you knew nothing about?

Raj: Well, not really. Sometimes I'm given something that I don't know much about, so I do some investigation and ask around, you know, to get up to speed.

5 Interviewer: Are you comfortable making decisions and taking the lead?

Raj: Yes, but not always. I think some decisions are better left to people more senior. For example, I don't like firing anyone.

🎧 **70**

1
Q: Tell me more about the project you mention on your CV, can you?
A: Erm, yeah, well, erm … I started it, let me see, about, erm, a year ago I guess. The purpose is to, to look at ways of increasing the company's income without adding additional cost. That's, that's very important. Most of our employees work shifts so, you know, we're looking at different things, um, like setting up a new shift pattern, maybe, and erm … ways of multi-tasking so that workers can cover for each other's absences and sickness. I guess you'd call that team building.

2
Q: Can you tell me about your responsibilities in your job at the moment?
B: Sure! I'm the Staff Development Supervisor, so that means I have to monitor staff performance and identify areas where skills need to be supplemented or improved. It's about designing and implementing training programmes, when and where they are needed, to make sure we get the most from our staff, and to make sure they are happy

too, of course! Actually, I established a new system to assess performance that seems to be very effective …

3
Q: Why do you want to work for this company?
C: Because, er, you lead the market in communications technology, and you have the best reputation of any company in the business. I like the corporate culture here. You're an ethical company, but you also, you know, are driven by profit. That's important. I want to work for the best. I think I'd be happy here. I'd need to relocate but that's fine. It's not far.

🎧 **71** (Speaker 1 = American)
Speaker 1
Er, well last year I tried to establish a new system for internal mail, but it was a complete disaster. I didn't take enough time to introduce it and nobody knew how it worked. I learned that although something seems clear to me, it doesn't mean that everyone else understands. I'll take more time and do more trials before I try anything like that again!

Speaker 2
Well, I enjoy the job I'm doing and I get on well with everyone, but I really want to move on and try something new. I've had this job for two years now and I think I've outgrown it. I'm ready for a new challenge, something that stretches me.

Speaker 3
I tend to worry too much whether the customer is satisfied or not, and that means sometimes I spend too much time on the customer and not enough time on other aspects of the job.

Review2

🎧 **72**
1 The printer won't print anything.
2 I asked over a month ago for a brochure.
3 So, you want four black ink VR10 cartridges and a box of 500 envelopes?
4 Would it be possible to speak to Kate Thomas, please?
5 Are you in the middle of something?
6 Shall we move on?
7 Can you give an example, perhaps?
8 Can we get back to the point here, please?
9 I'm a bit busy at the moment, I'm afraid.
10 What do you think I should do?

🎧 **73**
1
a I'm very sorry for the delay.
b Please give me a moment.
c I'd be grateful if you could be patient.
2
a Can I call you back?
b It might be worth checking the cables.
c I can't remember what it's called.

3
a Sorry, can I come in here?
b I have no problem with that.
c Certainly. I'll just put you through.
4
a Let me repeat that just to make sure.
b Can you run that by me again?
c It might be worth reducing our prices.
5
a I'd much rather have a late check out.
b I really must insist on a late check out.
c I'd appreciate it if you could arrange a late check out.
6
a I don't agree with that at all.
b The point I'm trying to make is …
c Can you go into a little more detail on …
7
a I'm not sure you've got that right.
b That's completely wrong.
c I didn't quite catch that.
8
a I'm sorry about this.
b Could you bear with me a moment, please?
c You'll have to wait.
9
a Would you mind speaking a little slower,
10 please?
b I didn't quite catch that. Can you run that by me again?
c I think we have a bad connection.

a No, sorry. I don't really go along with that.
b I'm afraid that's not really what I meant.
c Sorry. Can I just finish what I was saying?

Answer**key**

Unit**1**

Get ready to listen and speak
○ *Your own answers.*
○ If you like going to parties and meeting new people, then you are probably quite extrovert. If you prefer to socialize only with people you know, then you are more reserved. If you hate making small talk with strangers, switch off if you are not interested in a conversation, or prefer to listen to others, then your social style is more passive.

A
1 b work going   c see the news   d been hot today
e are the family   f like your jacket
2 2 e   3 a   4 f   5 d   6 b

B
1 b Nick   c Tim   d Nick   e Nick
2 Nick's conversation is more successful because he asks lots of questions, responds to information and sounds interested.

C
1 How long have you worked there?
Are you enjoying it?
2 *Your own answers. Possible answers*:
b What do you do? / Do you enjoy it?
c Where are you going? / How long are you going for?
d How long were you there?
e Where did you move to? / What's your new place like?
3 *Your own answers. Possible answers*:
b What do you do? / Do you like working in London?
c Where are you going? / How long will you be away for?
d Have you been working hard? / Didn't you sleep well last night?
e What was it? / Was it at the cinema or on TV?
f What kind of food do you like to cook? / Are you a good cook?
g How many years have you been married?
h What make is it? / A laptop or a desktop?

D
1 He asks her questions.
2 a down   b up
3 1 question b *is it*?   2 question a *isn't it*?
4 b It's great music, isn't it?
c It was cold yesterday, wasn't it?
d You've got two children, haven't you? / You have two children, don't you?
e They aren't from here, are they?   f It was your birthday last week, wasn't it?
5 b He hasn't found a job yet, has he?
c Julia didn't pass her driving test last week, did she?
d You're not going shopping next weekend, are you?
e They eat meat, don't they?
f You didn't watch the match last night, did you?

E
2 b Don't you?   c Have you?
4 *Your own answers. Possible answers*:
b Did it? What was the problem?
c Won't you? Where are you going?
d Aren't you? What's the problem/matter?
e Has he? That's great. When did you hear that?
f Is she? Do you know where she's going?
g Doesn't it? What's wrong with it?
h Didn't you? Why not?

Focus on question tags
1 b don't you   c isn't he
d is she   e haven't I
f don't they   g will you
h didn't we

Note: We add a negative question tag to a positive statement: *That was a great movie, wasn't it?*
We add a positive question tag to a negative statement: *You didn't see Miki, did you?*

F
1 a raining; play golf
b property prices; new flat
2 a disappointed   b 'Oh no. That's terrible'
3 a 2   b 1   c 3
4 What a pity!   c That's marvellous!   a How exciting!   b
5 That's marvellous!   c How exciting!   b

Focus on exclamations
b How awful!   c What a pity!   d What fantastic news!
e What a great idea!   f What appalling weather!   g How amazing!
h What a mess!   i How unusual!   j What a relief!!

Sound smart
b bored   c bored   d enthusiastic   e bored   f enthusiastic
g enthusiastic   h bored

Unit**2**

Get ready to listen and speak
○ b 10   c 3   d 6   e 9   f 1   g 7   h 2   i 11
j 4   k 12   l 5
○ *Your own answers.*

A
1 b digital camcorder   c plasma TV   d laptop/notebook computer
e all-in-one printer
2 b portable, on vacation, record video, take pictures
c a 50-inch screen, picture quality, watching movies, living room
d wireless, light, 80 gigabyte hard disk, 3 gigahertz processor, screen, software
e 24 pages a minute, black and white, a fax, can make copies

Answer key

B

1 b interested in   c you tell me what   d what does
e tell me about   f like to know   g What's; like

2 1 expressions c, d   2 expressions e, f, g   3 expressions a, b

3 2 store addresses and contacts   3 take notes and write documents
4 transfer files to your computer   5 read and send email
6 surf the Internet   7 take photos and videos
8 download video games   9 listen to music   10 watch TV

4 a You can connect to the Internet without having to plug into a computer.
b A 'hotspot' is an area where you can connect to the Internet.

Sound smart

2 cam<u>e</u>ra popul<u>a</u>r feat<u>u</u>re <u>a</u>ddress <u>a</u>ppointm<u>e</u>nt

4 a C<u>a</u>n I take <u>a</u> clos<u>e</u>r look?
b Here's <u>a</u> picture of me <u>a</u>nd my friend.
c The <u>a</u>ssistant said there's <u>a</u> sale on t<u>o</u>day.

C

3 *Your own answers. Possible answers:*
b Can I have a closer look, please?   c What happens if I press this button here?   d What is this keypad for?   e What does that blue button do?

D

1 Special payment terms, an extended warranty and delivery.

2 The special payment terms cost an extra $60. The extended warranty is $49.99, and the delivery charge is $40.

3 He buys the extended warranty. He does not have to pay for delivery.

E

1 *If you … then I …*

2 b If you give me 10% off, then I'll agree to the special payment terms.
c If you give free installation and demonstration, then I'll take the extended warranty.
d If you give me free delivery, then I'll sign up for the after-sales technical support.
e If you give me a discount, then I'll buy two.
f If you give me an extra battery, then I'll buy the leather case.

Focus on the language of sales

b off c on d on e for f in g down

F

1 Henri: a computer game   Pete: an all-in-one printer
Karen: a mobile phone

2 Henri   He already has this one.
Pete   It's faulty – the paper gets stuck and the fax doesn't work.
Karen   It crashes while on the Internet, and sometimes when she makes a call she can't hear anything.

G

2 You should tick all the expressions.
Jane says: *The thing is …*   Henri says: *The problem is …*
Pete says: *The problem seems to be …*   Karen says: *I don't understand why …*

3 *Your own answers. Possible answers:*
b I bought this camera last week but the problem is the screen doesn't work. Can I have a refund, please?
c This CD was a present but the the thing is I don't listen to music, really, so can I exchange it for something else, please?
d I got this computer game as a present but the thing is I already have it. Can I exchange it for a different one, please?
e I bought this DVD recorder last weekend but the remote control doesn't work. Can I exchange it for a different one, please?

Unit3

Get ready to listen and speak

Get ready to listen and speak

○ a 3 b 4 c 5 d 1 e 2 f 6
○ *Your own answers.*

A

1 b 3 c 4 d 1

2 b an appointment to see a doctor
c a check-up and their teeth polished
d to find out where his father is in the hospital

3 2 a 3 c 4 b

4 a Minor Injuries Unit   b £4.50   c an X-ray and check-up   d 4 pm

B

1 Step 1 fill in a **registration** form   Step 2 complete a **database** card
Step 3 have a **Well Person** Check

2 a her passport, and a letter from her school
b her health details, and details of her family's medical history

C

1 2 Seeing the nurse   3 Home visits   4 In an emergency
5 Asking for advice   6 Well Person Clinic   7 Special clinics
8 Repeat prescriptions

2/3
a False. The receptionist says you can 'drop in' (call in person) as well.
b False. We try to see everyone within two days.
c False. The nurse can give vaccinations also.
d True.
e False. They are only available between 11.30 and 12 on weekdays.
f True. On Wednesday and Friday afternoons
g True. The special clinics are for asthma, diabetes sufferers and a baby clinic for new mothers.
h True. The receptionist says they need 48 hours' notice.

D

1 2 B 3 B 4 A 5 B 6 A 7 B

2 Anne Bertrand
Treatment: *Nitropan **8**-week course.*
*One 1000mg tablet **in the morning** and another **at night***
Return visit **Yes**/No [If yes, when **in a month**]

Brian Kingston
Problem: **the flu (mild)**
Treatment: *Cordosole 5. 1-week course.*
2 x** 250mg tablets, 3x per day before **meals
Return visit Yes/**No** [If yes, when ....]

3 has stomach cramps, has diarrhoea, has been sick

4 *Your own answers.*

5 a She's got food poisoning.
b The doctor prescribes some tablets (two every four hours).
c No (only if she's not feeling better in a week).

E

1 She repeats the important information.

3 *Your own answers. Possible answers:*
b OK. So I need to take two spoonfuls after every meal.
c Right. So you're saying I have to just take one tablet in the morning and one at night.
d So you mean I should finish the course and then come back and see you if I'm not better.
e OK. So I need to eat less, avoid rich food and drink plenty of water.

100

2 b No, I have to take two tablets **after** each meal.
  c No, it's two spoonfuls **three** times a day.
  d No, I said I had a pain in my **right** arm.
  e No, I'm here to have a **blood test**.

Unit4

Get ready to listen and speak

○ 1 fuse 2 plug 3 cable 4 screw 5 screwdriver
  6 thermostat 7 switch 8 pipe
○ A battery can go flat. A pump can break.
  A printer cartridge can run out of ink. A computer can crash.
  A fuse can blow.

A

1 *Your own answers.*
2 Object   Problem
  a car   won't start
  b printer   won't print anything
  c washing machine won't spin
3 a This person decides to call the garage to have his car repaired.
  b This person decides to check the ink cartridge to make sure it hasn't run out.
  c This person decides to check whether the pump needs replacing.

Focus on modals of deduction

1 To make a deduction in the *present*, we use a modal of deduction and the infinitive.
  To make a deduction in the *past*, we use a modal of deduction + have + past participle.
2 a can't b must have c could have d might have
  e must have f might not

B

2 *Your own answers. Possible answers*:
  b The batteries might be flat. Perhaps they need replacing.
  c It could be the cartridge. It might have run out of ink.
  d It may be the thermostat. It might have broken.
  e It might be the fuse. I suppose it could have blown. I think you might need to buy a new fuse.
3 *Your own answers. Possible answers*:
  b No, it can't be a fuse either. I've checked them all already.
  c It's not the monitor, either. There's nothing wrong with the monitor.
  d No, it can't be the keyboard and mouse. I've put new batteries in.
  e Yeah. I suppose it must be the hard disk. It's the only thing I haven't checked. It can't be anything else.

C

1 You really shouldn't leave it any longer.
  You'd better call an electrician.
  You'd better not touch that cable. It might not be safe.
  You ought to call a plumber.
2 *Your own answers. Possible answers*:
  b You'd better call an electrician. You really shouldn't touch that cable.
  c You really should read the instructions again. You'd better not take it back yet.
  d You really should call an engineer. You'd better not take a look yourself.
  e You really should see a doctor. You shouldn't wait to see if it gets better.

3 *Your own answers. Possible answers*:
  b Well, you'd better not leave it or it may get worse.
  c You'd better not try to repair it yourself. You really should get a mechanic to have a look.
  d You really shouldn't use the car. You'd better go by train instead.
  e You'd better buy the ticket now. It might be busy tomorrow morning.

D

1 If you have a burglar alarm fitted, then this will act as a deterrent.
  You will be ill unless you eat more healthily.
  You should be more careful, otherwise you will have an accident.
2 *Your own answers. Possible answers*:
  b If you don't work hard, you'll fail your exams. / You'll fail your exams unless you work hard.
  c You should eat more healthily, otherwise you'll put on weight. / You'll put on weight unless you eat more healthily.
  d You should get it repaired, otherwise you'll fall behind with work. / You'll fall behind with work unless you get it repaired.
  e You should apologize, otherwise you might lose your job. / You might lose your job unless you apologize.

E

1 b 4 c 1 d 2
2 1 The lock on the door is broken, suggesting that the burglar came in through the door, but the woman says the burglar had *smashed a window and climbed through.*
  2 The smoke is coming through an open window but the man says it was *coming from under the front door.*
  3 The handbag is on the back seat of the car but the woman says the thief had *taken all my shopping bags and my handbag.* Also, the back door of the car is open, but the woman just says the thief *had smashed the back window.*
  4 There are two women in the car but the woman says she was *all on my own.*
3 2 a 3 d 4 b
4 *Your own answers.*

Unit5

Get ready to listen and speak

○ 1 passport 2 ID card 3 birth certificate 4 driving licence
  5 US social security card (allowing you to work and claim benefits if you are ill or unemployed) 6 residency permit
  7 work permit 8 entry visa 9 visa
○ *Your own answers.*

A

1 The number you need to press is 2.
2 *Your own answers. Possible answers*:
  website: www.ukvisas.gov.uk (download appl. forms + email Q)
  Fax number: 020 7008 8359
  Address: UK Visa section, London SW1A 2AH
  Opening hours: 9.30 am – 1.30 pm Mon to Fri (except pub. hols)

B

1 a 4 b 5 c 2 d 1 e 3 f 6
2 2 She has to fill out a form VAF1 and send it in with her passport, two recent color passport-sized photos and other necessary supporting documents.
  3 A letter of support from her school/college (e.g. saying what she'll be studying, how long the course is, etc.) and her last six months' bank statements.
  4 Part-time or holiday work is OK. Maximum 20 hours per week.
  5 A Student Visa is £85.
  6 She can apply by post or in person. She must apply between 1 and 3 months before she plans to go to the UK.

Answer key

C

1 Yuki uses the expression *What do you mean by …?*
3 *Your own answers. Possible answers*:
   2 Sorry, what's 'AIS'?   3 I'm sorry. I don't understand. What's a 'UK Mission'?   4 Sorry, can you explain what 'Schengen area' means, please?   5 What does 'EEA' mean?

D
1, 2

	Ways of obtaining a green card	Requirements
1	coming to work in the US, an employer-based green card	permanent job
2	have family there, a family-based green card	a family member in the US must be a citizen or already have a green card
3	win a green card through the Diversity Visa lottery program	must come from a country with a low rate of immigration to the US

3 a 1   b 4   c 3   d 2   e 5
4 birth certificate   biographical information   passport   two colour photos   fingerprints   a physical   a letter from your employer

E

1 a is better
2 *Your own answers. Possible answers*:
   1
   b That's because I really like it here. I'd like to stay here longer.
   c Just a few months. Less than nine for sure.
   d Yes, I've found a job in a supermarket.
   e Yes, I have. Here it is …
   2
   a I'm studying sociology.
   b I need the money to support myself while I study.
   c Another year.
   d Yes, I've found a job in a local restaurant. It's off campus so I need a work permit.
   e No, I haven't.

Unit6

Get ready to listen and speak

- a a statue   b a piazza/square   c a fountain   d a museum
  e a monument   f a park   g a beach/the seaside
  h a port   i a castle
- *Your own answers.*
- *Your own answers. Possible answers*:
  go to souvenir shops, visit a zoo, go to a theme park (i.e. Disneyland), walk around the 'old quarter' of a city, stop at cafés, have a picnic in a park, go to the theatre

A

1 Crosswell Hill is a park. Old Keller is a statue.
  The Typewriter is a monument. Figo's is a café or restaurant.
2 Crosswell Hill: walk / read (if weather's nice) / joggers / walking dogs
  Old Keller: huge / 100 feet high / an important person / made of marble
  The Typewriter: built after 2nd World War / names of men who died
  Figo's: eat / sandwiches / I'm starving!

B

1 *It's a good place to go if* you want to go dancing on a night out.
  It's handy for joggers.   *It's popular for* walking dogs.
  It's famous for its sandwiches.
2 *Your own answers. Possible answers*:
  museum – interesting   art gallery – beautiful paintings
  city centre – lovely old buildings   bars – great for a night out
  markets – great bargains
3 *Your own answers.*

C

1 b expensive   c get around   d What is there   e good beaches
  f biggest attraction   g nightlife   h famous for   i places to visit
  j best time
2 2 f   3 h   4 d   5 a   6 i   7 e   8 j   9 c   10 g
3 a False. The hotels aren't cheap.
  b True. The food is very varied and cosmopolitan.
  c False. You don't really need a car.
  d False. Alcatraz is 'well worth visiting'.
  e False. It's hardly ever hot enough to sunbathe.
  f True. It's generally quite mild.
  g True. The cable car is the 'best way to see the city'. There are lots of ferries and buses, too.
  h False. It's not famous for' nightlife, although there are some places to go.
4 The city Mark and the travel agent are talking about is San Francisco.

D

2 *You really ought to* (1)   *You have to* (2)   *should definitely* (3)
  You mustn't (2)   *well worth* (2) (with both a gerund *well worth visiting* and a noun *well worth a visit*)
3 *Your own answers. Possible answers*:
  b You should definitely visit the castle. It's fascinating.
  c The park is well worth a visit. It's absolutely wonderful.
  d You have to see the monument. It's huge!
  e You should definitely go to the beach. It's really beautiful.
4 *Your own answers. Possible answers*:
  b It's well worth buying a weekly tourist ticket. It's handy for using all the public transport.
  c You really ought to visit the park. You mustn't miss the Metropolitan Art Museum and there are lots of monuments worth seeing too.
  d You have to eat at Taki's Teriyaki Bar. It's a great place for really traditional food.

e   You should definitely go to Shibuya in the evening and check out the live music. The night markets are well worth going to as well.

f   If you can, you really ought to go in April because that's when the weather is best.

Review 1

Section 1
1 a 2 c 3 c 4 a 5 c 6 b 7 c 8 b 9 b 10 b

Section 2
1 a 2 c 3 a 4 b 5 c 6 a 7 b 8 a 9 c 10 b

Section 3
1 b 2 b 3 a 4 b 5 c 6 c 7 a 8 a 9 b 10 c

Section 4
Your own answers. Possible answers:

1 Oh really, did you? Why did you have to work? / What were you working on? / Did you finish everything?

2 You really should start revising. / If you don't start revising, you might fail. / You'll fail unless you do some work soon. You should do some work, otherwise you might fail.

3 Have I? That's fantastic! / That's absolutely wonderful. / Are you sure? / How did I win?

4 It could be the cable. / It might be the fuse. / You really should get someone to look at it. / You'd better not try to fix it yourself.

5 Oh yes? What are their names? / How old are they?

6 It was good, but it wasn't fantastic. / It was really boring.

7 Well, there's an art museum. It's a good place to go if it's raining. / You can find lots of great shops in the centre.

8 Yes, it's great. / I'm really enjoying it. How about you?

9 I'm sorry but can you explain what INS means, please? / I don't understand. What is the INS?

10 Have you? You should go to the dentist, otherwise it might get worse.

Unit 7

Get ready to listen and speak
○ a 1 b 3 c 1 d 4 e 2 f 2 g 4 h 2

A
1 b It will last five days (from the 5th to the 9th).

c Yes. There are several clues to the fact ARG held the same event there the previous year. (*There'll be 34 this time. It's full-board again.*)

d a whiteboard, a flipchart, delegate pads/pencils, water, wireless Internet access

2 Dates: July 5 – July 9 (inclusive)
Number of people: 37 (34, plus herself and two senior HR people)
Double rooms: 4
Requests / Special requirements:
– one delegate in wheelchair will need bedroom for disabled on ground floor
– as many rooms with baths as possible
– late check-out on 10th; 2pm
Study Centre: Shelly
Meeting room: C, E, F
Additional equipment: computer data projectors and screens
Catering: full-board
Refreshment breaks: 10.30am, 3.30 pm
Additional information: none

B
1 *I'd be grateful if you could* (give me a double room too …)
I'd appreciate it if you could (give us as many rooms with baths as you can.)

2 *Your own answers. Possible answers*:
b Can I ask you to make sure all rooms are on the ground floor?
c Could you possibly arrange the refreshment breaks for three o'clock each day, not half past three?
d I wonder if you could put fresh flowers in each room?
e I'd be grateful if you could make sure all rooms have an early morning call at seven every day.

3 *Your own answers. Possible answers*:
b Could you possibly turn up the air-conditioning in all the rooms?
c I'd appreciate it if you could get someone to repair the shower in room G29.
d I wonder if you could lend me a video camera tomorrow morning? I want to use it in Meeting Room C.
e Can I ask you to put some bottles of mineral water in all the training rooms, please?

C
1 I don't know what it's called but <u>you use it</u> to clean your teeth.
<u>I need something to</u> put these posters on a display board.
<u>Have you got anything for</u> cleaning marks off clothes?

2 1 b 2 c 3 a

3 *Your own answers. Possible answers*:
b My mobile phone is low on power. Have you got anything for recharging it?
c Yes please. I need something to cut up this paper.
d I don't know what it's called but you use it to add up numbers.

D
1 Viktor is reluctant to help. This is noticeable from his overall attitude and also the way he say *Hmm. Well, OK. I'll see if I can get anyone to help you out for a couple of days.*

2 a He's working on 'the London project'.
b It's a lot more work than he realized when he agreed to do it.
c He asks for some help to write up the report.
d He says he's in danger of falling behind, and may not finish on time.
e The deadline is a week on Friday.
f Viktor promises to find someone to help Peter for a couple of days.

> **Sound smart**
> 1 a angry/impatient b bored/uninterested c friendly/cooperative
> 3 friendly/cooperative 3, 8 angry/impatient 1, 7
> bored/uninterested 2, 4, 5, 6

E
2 Peter uses all of the expressions.

3 *Your own answers. Possible answers*:
b If would help a lot if someone could explain how to use the new database. I'm in danger of making mistakes.
c I could really do with a new printer. The reports may not be clear enough if I don't print in colour.
d It would help a lot if someone could help me photocopy the reports. I'm in danger of not finishing on time.
e I could really do with a holiday soon. I may become ill if I don't take a break.

> **Focus on interrupting**
> 2 2 f 3 b 4 c 5 a 6 d

Unit8

Get ready to listen and speak
- a 1 b 6 c 4 d 7 e 3 f 5 g 2
- Your own answers.

A
1 Established: 1989
Main activity: provides microchip technology to computer manufacturers
Headquarters: Cambridge   Turnover: over £250 million
No of employees: 1100 worldwide   Current market share: 15%
2 b
the best products – Quality / the most competitive prices – Prices /
in the quickest time frame – Speed
3 b   President   c   Human Resources   d   R and D
e   Technical Support   f   Sales and Marketing

B
2 Your own answer. Possible answer:
Drucher Bahn Systems was established in 1862. It is one of the leading manufacturers of railway vehicles in the world. It is at the forefront of technology in its field. The carriages it manufactures are 20% lighter than the competition. It has enjoyed rapid growth in recent years and has an annual turnover of 575 million euros. It has around 15 per cent of the market. Over 12 thousand people work for the company, which is based in Berlin, in Germany. It is headed by Hans Kilmer, the Managing Director. The company is organized into five divisions; Operations, Production, Business Development, HR and Finance. The Operations division includes two departments, Design and Maintenance. The Business Development division is made up of the Strategy and Project Management departments.
3 Your own answer. Refer to the example above as a model.

C
1 Let me introduce you to our General Manager.
Can I introduce you to Sonya?
I'd like you to meet our new marketing director.
I want you to meet the rest of the team.
2 You hear: This is … / Let me introduce you to… / I want you to meet …
3 Carol Parks: Accounts Manager   Tim Starks: Payroll Manager
Helen Green: CFO
All these people work in the Finance Department.

Focus on job titles
2 Chief Executive Officer   3 Chief Financial Officer
4 Vice President   5 Chief Information Officer
6 Chief Operations Officer

D
1 Carl a   Youssry c   Heidi e
2 Carl: expenditure / investments / budget allocation / resource management.
Youssry: people / hiring and firing / welfare and professional development / staff
Heidi: design new technologies / research and study / practical testing and trials

E
2 Your own answers. Possible answers:
They all need to be flexible, efficient, reliable, good with computers, etc.
Michiko: creative, able to meet deadline, good at communicating
Carl: analytical, good at solving problems
Youssry: sociable, good at communicating, a good listener
Heidi: analytical, methodical
3 Your own answers.

Sound smart
1 a There are five syllables in *analytical*.
b The main stress is on the middle syllable as shown by the stress pattern ooOoo.
2

oOo	Ooo	oOoo
creative	flexible	methodical
efficient	confident	reliable
determined	sociable	well-organized

F
1 Michiko uses *I'm in charge of …* / *My main responsibility is to …*
Carl uses *My job involves …* / *I'm mainly concerned with …*
Youssry uses *I'm interested in …* / *I'm responsible for …*
Heidi uses *My job involves …*
2 Your own answers.

Focus on prepositions with work
2 in   3 with   4 in   5 on   6 to

Unit9

Get ready to listen and speak
- a 6 b 5 c 4 d 3 e 2 f 1
- Your own answers.
- Your own answers.

A
1
Conversation 1
The assistant promises to process the order and send the book.
The customer is not satisfied because the book hasn't been sent yet and the assistant can't guarantee when it will be sent.

Conversation 2
The problem is the wrong printer cartridges were delivered.
The assistant promises to post the correct cartridges by special delivery, and gives the customer a £30 credit.
The customer seems very satisfied.

2 b   very busy recently   c   I'll check   d   immediately   e   the mix-up
f   computer problems   g   a moment   h   right away

B
1 ask someone to be patient: c, g   apologize: a, e
promise to take action: d, h   explain the cause of a problem: b, f
2 Your own answers. Possible answers:
b   I see. I'm very sorry for the delay. I'm afraid we've been very busy this month.
c   I'm very sorry for the inconvenience. Unfortunately we're having problems with our website.
d   Oh, I do apologize. I'm afraid there has been an administrative error.
e   Oh dear. I'm very sorry. Unfortunately the manager is ill today.
3 Your own answers. Possible answers:
b   I do apologize. I'll sort it out right away. I'll book an engineer to fix it.
c   I'm very sorry for the mix-up. I'll get onto it immediately. I'll arrange to exchange it for the right one.
d   I do apologize. I'll sort this out for you immediately. I'll refund the 15%.
e   I'm very sorry. I'll get onto this right away. I'll ask someone to call you.

4 *Your own answers. Possible answers*:
  b Please give me a moment and I'll check. Yes, we should be getting some more in next Monday.
  c Yes, I'll send one special delivery as soon as we have them.
  d You're welcome. Goodbye.

C

2 *Your own answers. Possible answers*:
  b You want to order a pair of blue Extra-light trainers, is that correct?
  c You want to order a plasma screen 32-inch TV, at £949, is that right?
  d You want to order a 5-piece Analon saucepan set, is that correct?
  e You want to order a red Valencia sofa and you'd like it to be delivered on Monday 1st June, is that right?

> **Sound smart**
> 2 a I /j/ asked you /w/ over a month ago for a brochure.
>   b Please give me /j/ a moment to check.
>   c I'll get onto /w/ it immediately.
>   d We'll post the /j/ order special delivery.
>   e I'll post it in the /j/ afternoon.
>   f Can I /j/ ask who /w/ is speaking, please?
>   g I do /w/ apologize for all the /j/ inconvenience.
>   h You sent me /j/ an email to /w/ ask about delivery.
>   i I'll be /j/ out of the /j/ office all next week.

D

1 a 4 b 2 c 5 d 6 e 3
2 b keeps crashing c print anything
  d go through e doesn't work f record anything
3 *Your own answers.*
4 2 a 3 f 4 b 5 e 6 d
5 a The problem is that the photocopier won't work.
  b They open the copier and look inside.
  c Some paper was stuck inside.

E

1 It might be worth opening it; You could try pulling that …
2 Have you tried switching it off … What about pressing the …
3 *Your own answers. Possible answers*:
  b Have you tried asking a technician to look at it?
  c It might be worth reducing our prices.
  d What about having a special promotion?
  e You could try giving the staff a bonus.
  f It might be worth changing supplier.

Unit 10

> **Get ready to listen and speak**
> ○ *Your own answers.*
> ○ Do sound relaxed   Don't eat while you speak
>   Do be polite   Don't use slang words
>   Don't speak quickly   Do speak clearly
>   Don't rush the conversation Do sound friendly
>   Do speak naturally   Don't continue to work while talking
> ○ *Your own answers.*

A

1 Conversation 1
  b He's in a meeting. c He should be free after lunch.
  d He asks that Mr Fredericks calls him because it's important.

  Conversation 2
  e The Accounts Department. f Because he needs to check some figures. g Because she's out of the office. h To tell her that he has called.

2 b Would it be possible to speak to Mr Fredericks, please?
  c Will he be available this afternoon? d Could you ask him to call me? e Thanks very much. Goodbye.
3 2 e 3 a 4 d 5 c
4 2 Is Sharon there? 3 Do you know when she'll be back?
  4 When she gets in can you say …? 5 Thanks a lot. Bye.
5 Conversation 1 is more formal. Full names are used, and polite questions.

> **Focus on telephoning**
> b at c in d in e through f on g from h back

B

1 a 5 b 6 c 1 d 3 e 2 f 4
2 *Your own answers. Possible answers*:
  b I see. Will she be available this afternoon?
  c Could you ask her to call me as soon as possible?
  d [your name] from Suntours international. My mobile number is 07967 324094.
  e Thanks very much. Goodbye.
3 *Your own answers. Possible answers*:
  b Do you know when she'll be back? c OK. Can you say I called?
  d I'm on extension 344. e Thanks a lot. Bye.

C

1 Conversation 2 is more formal. Full names are used, and polite questions.
2 2 a message 3 try 4 line's engaged 5 This is
  6 Would you like 7 you through 8 on another call
3 a 1,5 b 4,8 c 3,7 d 2,6

D

1 a 2 b 6 c 1 d 4 e 5 f 3
2 *Your own answers. Possible answers*:
  b I'm afraid she's on another line right now.
  c Would you like to leave a message?
  d Certainly. Can I ask who's calling?
  e That's fine. I'll make sure she gets the message. Thanks for calling.
3 *Your own answers. Possible answers*:
  b No, sorry. The line's engaged.
  c Can I take a message?
  d Sure. No problem. Samantha, isn't it?
  e OK. I'll pass that on for you. Bye for now.

> **Sound smart**
> 3 b 11 words (the contraction you're counts as two words, *you are*)
>   c 8 d 7 e 8

E

1 *Your own answers. Possible answer*:
  The man is on a busy street, with a lot of noise from traffic in the background.
2 1 b 2 c 3 a 4 e 5 d
3 b run that by me c speak up d bad connection e a little slower
4 *Your own answers. Possible answers*:
  b Can/Could you speak/Would you mind speaking a little slower, please?
  c Sorry. Can you run that by me again?
  d Would you mind spelling / Do you think you could spell that for me?
  e I think we have a bad connection. I'll call you back.

Answer key

Unit 11

Get ready to listen and speak
- *Your own answers.*
- *Your own answers. Possible answers*:
  - read the agenda in advance
  - ensure everyone has the chance to participate
  - keep the meeting on track (not allowing too many digressions)

A
1 b let me thank   c especially like to   d purpose of   e can see from
2 2 a 3 c 4 b 5 d
3 *Your own answers. Possible answers*:
Other expressions might include
- a getting everyone's attention
  OK, everyone. Are we ready to start?
  Can we start?
- b thanking people
  May I take this opportunity to thank everyone for being here today? I'd glad you could all make it.
- c welcoming people
  I'd like to introduce everyone to …
- d explaining the aims of the meeting
  The main reason we're here is to …
  I've called this meeting because …
- e referring people to the agenda
  If you look at the agenda you'll see …
  We have five main items to discuss, …

4 b False. Ian has also come from Spain.   c True   d True   e False
There are *several items to cover*.

B
1

	Agrees	Disagrees	Partly agrees
David			✓
Inessa	✓		
Javier			✓
Ian		✓	

2 b I'm not completely opposed to it.   c I can see pros and cons each way.   d I'm in favour of it.   e I'm not very keen on the idea at all.
3 2 I see your point, but …
3 Perhaps we should consider …
4 I have no problem with that.
5 I can't agree to that, I'm afraid.
4 b 1 c 4 d 3 e 5

Focus on the language of meetings
2 g 3 h 4 b 5 a 6 d 7 e 8 f

C
1 1 a, e 2 b, g 3 h, j 4 c, f 5 d, i
2 Could you let [Javier] finish, please?
Does anyone have anything else to add?
Shall we move on?
3 *Your own answers. Possible answers*:
- b I think we need to look at this in more detail. / Perhaps we should discuss this a bit more.
- c I'm not sure that holiday entitlement is relevant here. / I think we're drifting off the point a bit.
- d Shall we move on? / OK. Does anyone have anything else to add?
- e Let's go over what we've agreed. / OK, to sum up then …

Sound smart
1 a We need to <u>expand</u> our European operations, not <u>close</u> them <u>down</u>!
… say the relevant words (louder)/ softer than the other words.
3 a Sales should be <u>increasing</u>, not <u>falling</u>.
- b We need our staff to work <u>longer</u> hours, not <u>shorter</u>.
- c We should be <u>hiring</u> staff, not <u>firing</u> them.
- d We need more <u>skilled</u> labour, not <u>unskilled</u> labour.
- e We need to be more <u>competitive</u>, not more <u>expensive</u>.

D
1 2 c 3 a 4 d
2 These meetings <u>don't tend</u> to be particularly <u>useful</u>.
Strategies 1 and 4

<u>Would you agree that</u> <u>on the whole</u>, our performance <u>wasn't very good</u>?
Strategies 1, 3 and 4
3 *Your own answers. Possible answers*:
- b On the whole sales haven't been very good.
- c Customers tend to think the quality isn't very good.
- d In general, would you agree that the senior management might be to blame?
- e On the whole, the company's reputation may have suffered slightly.

Unit 12

Get ready to listen and speak
- *Your own answers.*
- *Your own answers.*

A
1 Do: decide what is important; use abbreviations/symbols/numbers; organize your notes effectively; try and predict what you will hear; listen for the main ideas; rewrite your notes asap
Don't: note everything; write everything in full; panic if you miss something
2 a She says a lecture is not a dictation.
- b Before the lecture you should ask yourself what you already know about the topic. During the lecture you need to think about where the talk might be heading.
- c By paraphrasing and summarizing.
- d To review notes effectively you need to rewrite them, reorganize them, highlight the main points and add your own thoughts/comments.
- e The two advantages she mentions are that this will help everything sink in and also provide a useful study aid.

Focus on arrows, symbols and abbreviations
1 1 +   9 ↓
2 e.g.   10 ✓
3 imp.   11 poss
4 etc.   12 temp.
5 msg   13 vs.
6 ↑   14 =
7 ✗   15 info
8 C   16 yr.
2 *Your own answers.*
3 *Your own answers.*

B

1 2 b 3 b 4 b 5 b

2 *Your own answers. Possible answers*:

Background to economic success
Mass. econ growth / last 40 yrs / most signif geopol event 21stC. late 70s (econ rfms)

Growth statistics
Grown av. 10% pa / Exports ↑
Ind prod 17% pa. ↑
>2001, 2x glob. Man. output.
No. 2, but will overtake US nt 10yrs.

A population on the move
pop. 1.3bn.
200m people rural → urban areas
middle class ↑

Economic deficiencies
many manufac. comps
foreign
wages poss. ↑

Future challenges
must ↑ investment in skills + training
must produce own experts + entrepreneurs

3 *Your own answers. Refer to the answers above as a model.*

C

2 *Your own answers. Possible answers*:
The talk was about China's economy. The speaker began by talking about the emergence of China as a major economic power, which started with economic reforms in the late 1970s. Then she gave some statistics about China's economy today. It's the second-largest in the world, and should overtake the US in a few years. She went on to talk about China's population, and the migration from rural to urban areas.
She then talked about some possible weaknesses in the Chinese economy, like the fact that if wages rise, China might become less attractive to foreign companies. Finally, she talked about the challenges facing China's economy, in particular the need for China to produce its own experts and entrepreneurs in the future.

D

1 Summary a is better.

2 *Your own answers. Possible answers*:
Summary a
Strengths: This covers all the main points. It is well-organized and accurate, and uses a variety of appropriate signposts (words like: Then …, Finally etc.), including some useful detail.
Weaknesses: There are no specific statistics, and the speaker does not explain why dependence on foreign companies may be a problem in the future.
Summary b
Strengths: Some useful information covered, together with the main points. Signposts are OK.
Weaknesses: It misses a lot of information, e.g. background and fails to mention relevant details, e.g. says China's economy is still not the biggest, rather than is second behind the US, which is more informative. It is vague, e.g. millions rather than 200 million. There is nothing on the challenges for the future.

E

1 *Your own answers. Possible answers*:
b cost of labour c middle class = 'backbone of China's success'
d impact of China's economic growth

2 2 a 3 b 4 d

3 b driving at c trying to make d saying

F

1 b Can you go into a bit more detail on …?
c What exactly are you getting at when you …?
d Would you expand a little on …?

2 *Your own answers. Possible answers*:
b Could/Can you go explain what you mean by economic superpower?
c What exactly are you getting at when you refer to the 'draining effect' of migration from countryside to cities?
d Would you expand a little on the environmental cost of economic success?
e Could/Can you go explain what you mean by skill shortage?
f Can you go into a bit more detail on the causes of rising inflation?

Unit 13

Get ready to listen and speak

○ Slide a is a line graph, slide b a pie chart and slide c is a bar chart.

A

1 a 2 b 1 c 3

2 a International visitor arrivals
b The importance of the Australian market
c Reasons for travel to New Zealand

3 a Australia, the UK, the Americas, North-East Asia.
b Low airfares and aggressive marketing by New Zealand's Ministry for Tourism.
c The predicted rate of growth is 3% per annum (per year).
d Most tourists are interested in sightseeing and outdoor activities.
e VFR means Visiting Friends and Relatives.

Focus on describing statistics

1 b 4 c 5 d 2 e 6 f 1 g 7 h 3
2 2 e 3 f 4 a 5 c 6 b

B

1 b this chart c shows d can see e As you f draw

2 See the audioscript for suggestions on how to describe the slides on page 60.

3 *Your own answers. Possible answers*:
Visitor arrivals
You'll notice that the most popular months for visitors to come to New Zealand are between November and the end of March. You can see from this graph that there is almost no change in the popularity of each month year after year. Numbers increase sharply from November, reach a peak in December, and then drop slowly from there. The least popular months are from May to the end of September.

Total expenditure
You can see from this graph that the total expenditure of tourists in New Zealand was level between 1988 and 1994, but then increased dramatically to 1995. It levelled out briefly before a brief drop and since 1996 tourism expenditure has been increasing steadily. It levelled out in 2002 but forecasts up to 2012 show a steady rise is expected.

Growth in visitor arrivals
Now, this chart shows the forecast up to 2012. You can see that the percentage increase in numbers will remain steady at around four per cent until 2011 when a sharp rise is expected, which will fall in 2112 to around 3 per cent. Looking back, the biggest rises in tourists coming to New Zealand have been in 1994, 2000 and 2004. There were slight negative growth periods in 1991, 1997 and 1998.

Answer key

Sound smart

2 If you want to list several points one after the other, your voice should go (up) / *down* on the first two examples, and then go *up* / (down) on the final example.

4 a Great Britain is made up of three countries; England, Scotland and Wales.

 b Wales is popular for walking, its great beaches and its many castles.

 c In Scotland tourists visit Edinburgh, Loch Ness and enjoy the great scenery.

 d Popular tourist destinations in England are the Lake District, Cornwall and of course London.

 e London's top attractions include the London Eye, the Tower of London and Buckingham Palace.

 f Three popular musems are the National Gallery, the British Museum and the Tate Modern.

C

1 Linking supporting ideas: in addition, also, furthermore, moreover
 Contrasting different ideas: although, whereas, despite, however

2 *Your own answers. Possible answers:*
 b However, you'll notice that in May whereas sales continue to rise, profits fell.
 c I'd like to draw your attention to the figures for our turnover. You can see from this chart that although domestic turnover has increased from 4 million last year to 4.5 million this year, international turnover has fallen from 3.7 million last year to 3.2 million this year.
 d You can see here that salaries have continued to rise for managers and also workers.
 e What we can see here is our performance as regards customer service. Interestingly, despite fewer complaints the level of returns has remained the same.

Focus on expressing contrast
b in spite of c However d Although e whereas
f Even though

D

1 *Your own answers.*
2 *Your own answers.*
 The expressions you hear are:
 a As a result … b For example … c In other words …
 d To sum up, then …
3 *Your own answers.*

E

1 1 b, f 2 c, e 3 a, d
2 *Your own answers. Possible answers:*
 b Right, I've told you about productivity so let's move on to profit. The crucial point here is that corporation tax has gone up by 2%.
 c Now we've looked at staff levels let me turn to salaries. The thing to remember here is that there have been no pay rises for two years.
 d OK, I've told you about domestic marketing. Now let's move on to international marketing. The crucial point is that here we can see some big cultural differences.
 e We've looked at the workforce. Now let's turn to the management. The thing to remember here is that there are currently far fewer women than men in managerial positions.

Unit 14

Get ready to listen and speak
 a T b T c T d T
 Your own answers.

A

1 c
2 a The discussion is fairly well-balanced. Three people are in favour of protecting languages and two people don't agree.
 b It's a bit of both. The discussion starts strongly in favour of protecting languages, then reservations and counter arguments are made and things become increasingly heated. The discussion never becomes hostile, though. A good seminar *should* involve lively discussion!
 c Not completely. Three speakers (A, D and E) do most of the talking.
3 a 5 b 1 c 3 d 4 e 2
4 a According to the UNESCO report, there are more than 6000 languages in the world today, and over half are in danger of dying out by 2100.
 b Speakers of the Ainu language come from Japan. Speakers of the Maori languages live in New Zealand.
 c In 1991, only 19% of the population of Wales spoke Welsh. Today it's around 25%.
 d The arguments in favour of language revitalization are: languages tell us about who we are; you can't separate language from culture.
 e The arguments against language revitalization are: it might be natural for languages to become extinct; speaking the same language might help global understanding; the cost of protecting minority languages is high; the money could be spent on saving people from starvation and disease.

B

1 2 a 3 b 4 a
2 *Your own answers. Possible answers:*
 b I think you might be mistaken on that point. I think it's over 3,500 years ago.
 c I don't think you've got that right. I think a third of all languages are African languages.
 d I think you might be mistaken on that point. I think it's written from top to bottom and right to left.
 e I don't think you've got that right. I think it's Basque.
 f I think you might be mistaken on that point. I think they speak Portuguese.
3 *Your own answers. Possible answers:*
 b I don't quite see it like that. I think it depends on the individual.
 c I'm not sure I agree. I think it's too expensive to do that.
 d I don't quite see it like that. I think it would be less interesting.
 e I'm not sure I agree. I think language and culture are closely connected.
 f I'm not sure I agree. I think more people are learning English.

Sound smart
1 B sounds more polite. The speaker's voice is softer and calmer.
2 I'm not sure you've got that right. B That's not quite how I see it. A
 I'm not sure I agree. A Sorry, can I finish what I was saying? B

C

1 I'd like to hear more about the …
 Do you have any specific details about the …
 Can you give an example of a …

2 *Your own answers. Possible answers*:

    b Can you give an example of any endangered languages?

    c Do you think you could say a bit more about language revitalization?

    d Do you have any specific details about the rate of decline of minority languages?

    e I'd like to hear more about the threats to African languages, if possible.

    f Do you think you could say a bit more about the future of language development?

D

1/2   2 Basically 3 asking 4 another 5 suppose

3 a 3 b 1 c 5 d 4 e 2

E

1 b of what you've c go along with d really do think

    e the way I feel f back to the point g got it wrong

    h what I meant i you're saying j you think k finish what I

    l say something

2 1 j 2 a 3 l 4 k 5 g 6 f 7 e 8 c 9 b 10 i

    11 h 12 d

3 *Your own answers. Possible answers*:

    1 What's your opinion? / Do you agree with …?

    2 Can you go over that? Could you say what you mean?

    3 Can I add a point here? / Do you mind if I interrupt?

    4 I'd rather you waited until I've finished. / Can you let me finish?

    5 Sorry, I misunderstood.

    6 I think we're drifting off the point slightly.

    7 You're right. / Yes, I agree (completely).

    8 I don't agree (at all). / I think you're mistaken/wrong.

    9 I don't completely disagree but … / That's a good point but …

    10 Let me see if I've understood correctly. / Am I right in thinking …

    11 You didn't understand what I said.

    12 I'm absolutely sure/convinced that … / I strongly believe that …

Unit 15

Get ready to listen and speak

- *Your own answers.*
- *Your own answers.*
- *Your own answers.*

A

They feel that studying will benefit their employment prospects.
They are both interested in having international careers.
They both want to develop their language skills.

B

2 Stefania says: I plan to … / My main goal is to … / I expect … will … help me to

    Habib says: I intend to / I hope it'll help me to / that's the main purpose / I hope to

3 *Your own answer. Possible answer*:

    I plan to go to San Francisco Language Center next summer, for two months, on their American Language and Culture Program. I'll stay with a host family while I'm there. My main goal is to improve my English. I'll have 26 hours of tuition every week and get lots of practice in communication skills. I hope it'll help me to become more confident when I speak in English. I also expect I'll learn about American culture and get to know the people better and the lifestyle. It'll be fun to make friends with people from all around the world, too. What I hope to get from this is a better understanding of the language and culture of the United States.

C

2 *Your own answers. Possible answers*:

    b Do you think I should stay for one month or two months?

    c What do you think of going to London, or maybe Cambridge?

    d Do you think it's worth staying with a host family, or should I stay in a hotel?

    e Would you recommend studying for 15 hours a week or 28 hours a week?

    f Do you think I should study General English or for an exam like IELTS or TOEFL?

    g What do you think of going to the US or Australia instead?

D

1 b F (They will not be considered if they are handed in late.) c T

    d F (Students must do a 15-minute oral.) e F (There are 23.) f

    T

2 Grading system

    30% Final exam   20% Written assignments

    10% Oral report   10% Preparedness/participation

    Grades

    A 90+   B 80–90   C 70–80   D 60–70   F 59 or below

3 a Each written report represents 5% of the final grade. (There are four reports and together they make up 20%. Each report has 'equal weighting')

    b The exams are organized in two parts. A multiple choice test and then four short essay questions.

    c The oral report takes the form of a 15-minute presentation (on a topic of the student's choice related to the main course themes), followed by a Question and Answers session also of 15 minutes.

    d Students need to attend at least 80% in order to pass. As there are 23 classes, if they miss more than four classes they will fail.

E

1 The Library closes at *5*pm on Saturday. It is *not* open on Saturday out of term time, and there is no admittance *15* minutes before closing.

2 b rare books and manuscripts c main catalogue

    d special collections

3 a The Reading Room and the North Wing b a password c books published before 1978

4 2nd year students   N/A

    3rd year students   5 books for up to 8 weeks

    Academics   10 books for up to 8 weeks

    Research students   10 books for up to 8 weeks

F

1 *Your own answers.*

2 b where to find a book c access the Internet d make copies

    e have the book I want f overdue books g clear away books

    h using the library

3 2 e 3 h 4 d 5 b 6 a 7 f 8 g

4 a True. Wi-Fi hotspots are 'dotted around the place'.

    b True. £5 for university members, £10 for others.

    c True. You just need to 'sign up'.

    d False. Only if it's a journal and you need permission.

    e False. 'You'll soon get used to it'.

    f False. It's called Library Services.

    g False. There are 'virtually no exceptions'.

    h False. If you use a Retainer slip, staff won't take it away.

Answer key

Sound smart

1 The speaker's voice goes up at the end of questions a and c.
   The speaker's voice goes down at the end of questions b and d.
2 Questions that have a *Yes/No* answer usually have rising intonation.
   Questions that begin *Wh-* usually have falling intonation.
3 The intonation rises at the end of these questions:
   c Can I access the Internet on my laptop?
   d Can I make copies?
   g Do staff clear away books every evening?
   h Can I get any help on using the library?

   The intonation falls at the end of these questions:
   a How exactly do I go about searching for a book?
   b How do I know where to find a book once I have its location?
   e What if the library doesn't have the book I want?
   f What's the charge for overdue books?

Unit 16

Get ready to listen and speak

○ *Your own answers. Suggested answers*:
   Don't appear interested only in the salary and benefits.
   Don't appear over-confident or superior.
   Do arrive punctually.
   Don't criticize your current employer or colleagues.
   Do dress smartly.
   Don't look at the wall or floor when you talk.
   Don't mumble or fail to finish sentences.
   Do research the company beforehand.
   Do show enthusiasm.
   Do tailor your CV to fit the job.
○ *Your own answers.*

A

1 Maria refer to 6 tips (in order):
   Do research the company / tailor your CV to fit the job / dress smartly / arrive punctually / show enthusiasm
   Don't appear over-confident or superior.
2 Talk about any relevant work experience.
   Mention any qualifications that relate to the job.
   Mention any skills or special training you have.
   Explain what you can bring to the organization.
3 Mark gives the best response. (See below for details.)
4 Juan: This is OK, but there are some irrelevancies and not enough detail.
   Good points: gives some academic background and work experience, including current position. Talks briefly about some skills. Gives an idea of why he wants the job. Bad points: no indication of type/level of qualifications. Fails to expand in enough detail on his experience, or show how his experience might help the company. Talks about personal life and hobbies.

   Mark: This is clear, logical and concise. He covers all the main points well and sounds enthusiastic.
   Good points: gives appropriate details of academic background and work experience. He explains why he wants the job, what he can bring to the organization and also hints at the positive effect he could have.
   Bad points: he could expand in more detail on exactly how his MBA has helped him (i.e. what marketing strategies in particular he has used effectively).

   Amelia: This is the weakest of the three.
   Good points: gives some ideas of personal qualities and skills.
   Bad points: disjointed and illogical order, no academic details, poor explanation of her experience and no attempt to relate this to the job, irrelevant personal details.

B

2 Juan b, c   Mark a, e   Amelia d
3 *Your own answers.*
4 *Your own answers. See audioscript for possible answers.*

Focus on personal qualities and skills

1 2 d 3 a 4 e 5 b
2 well-organized P opinionated N boastful N strong-minded P domineering N tactful P creative P vain N determined P
3 *Your own answers.*

C

1 a 5 b 1 c 4 d 2 e 3
2 1 e 2 c 3 b 4 a 5 d
3 2 Good 3 OK 4 Poor 5 Poor
4 *Your own answers. Possible answers.*
   1 Raj gives a good example of how he is organized (using a filing system) and answers the question fully.
   2 Raj explains the problem clearly, and why it was important (the company was losing a lot of money). He showed he worked hard to overcome the problem independently.
   3 Raj describes the problem clearly, and the solution he came up with solved it easily to everyone's benefit. However, he does not explain how he convinced the management and workers to accept the changes (i.e. exactly how he used interpersonal skills).
   4 Raj points out his ability to research new areas independently, and shows initiative in asking colleagues. However, he doesn't give a concrete example so it is very vague and lacks the necessary detail to satisfy the interviewer.
   5 Raj clearly indicates his preference to leave difficult decisions to others.

Sound smart

1 The most confident speaker is Speaker 2.
   Speaker 2 speaks clearly, not too quickly, and pauses where appropriate. Her pronunciation is good and her stress and rhythm sound natural. She doesn't speak too quietly or mumble (Speaker 3) and she doesn't hesitate (Speaker 1) or speak too fast. She manages to come across as lively and enthusiastic.
3 *Your own answers.*

D

1 Speaker 1 Tell me about a time you failed badly at something.
   Speaker 2 If you like your current job, why do you want to leave?
   Speaker 3 What do you think is your greatest weakness?
2 a Speaker 2
   b Speaker 3
   c Speaker 1
3 *Your own answers.*

Review 2

Section 1
1 c 2 b 3 c 4 c 5 a 6 a 7 c 8 a 9 c 10 a
Section 2
1 a 2 b 3 c 4 b 5 c 6 c 7 a 8 b 9 b 10 c
Section 3
1 b 2 a 3 b 4 c 5 b 6 a 7 c 8 b 9 c 10 c

Section 4

Possible answers:

1 Oracle Inc was founded twenty years ago. It is based in Sweden. Its main activities are computer chip manufacturing and electronics. It has a turnover of around five million dollars. It is headed by …

2 Could you possibly let me have a room with a bath rather than a shower? / I'd be grateful if you could give me a room with a bath. / I wonder if you could find a room with a bath for me?

3 I'm in favour of it. / I can see pros and cons each way. / To some extent I agree. / I'm not very keen on the idea at all.

4 Have you got anything for cleaning marks off clothes? / I need something to get this mark off my jacket. / I don't know what it's called but it's a liquid you use to clean marks off clothes.

5 I'm well-organized, determined, reliable and I can work well under pressure. I enjoy communicating with people and I'm a good listener, too.

6 Would it be fair to say that the latest sales campaign was not a great success? / On the whole, I think the results were rather disappointing.

7 Lizzie, John. I want you to meet Mr Stevens. He's just joined us. He's our new marketing manager. / Mr Stevens. I'd like you to meet two of my colleagues. Lizzie and John. / John? Lizzie? This is Mr Stevens. He's the new marketing manager.

8 I could really do with a hand to move this cabinet. / It would help a lot if you could give me a hand to move this filing cabinet.

9 I work in the Accounts department. My job involves making sure that the company operates within budget. My main responsibility is to keep expenses down.

10 Sorry to disturb you. Have you got a minute? It's rather urgent. / Are you in the middle of something?

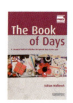